COLORING FUN
WITH
GEOMETRIC DESIGNS

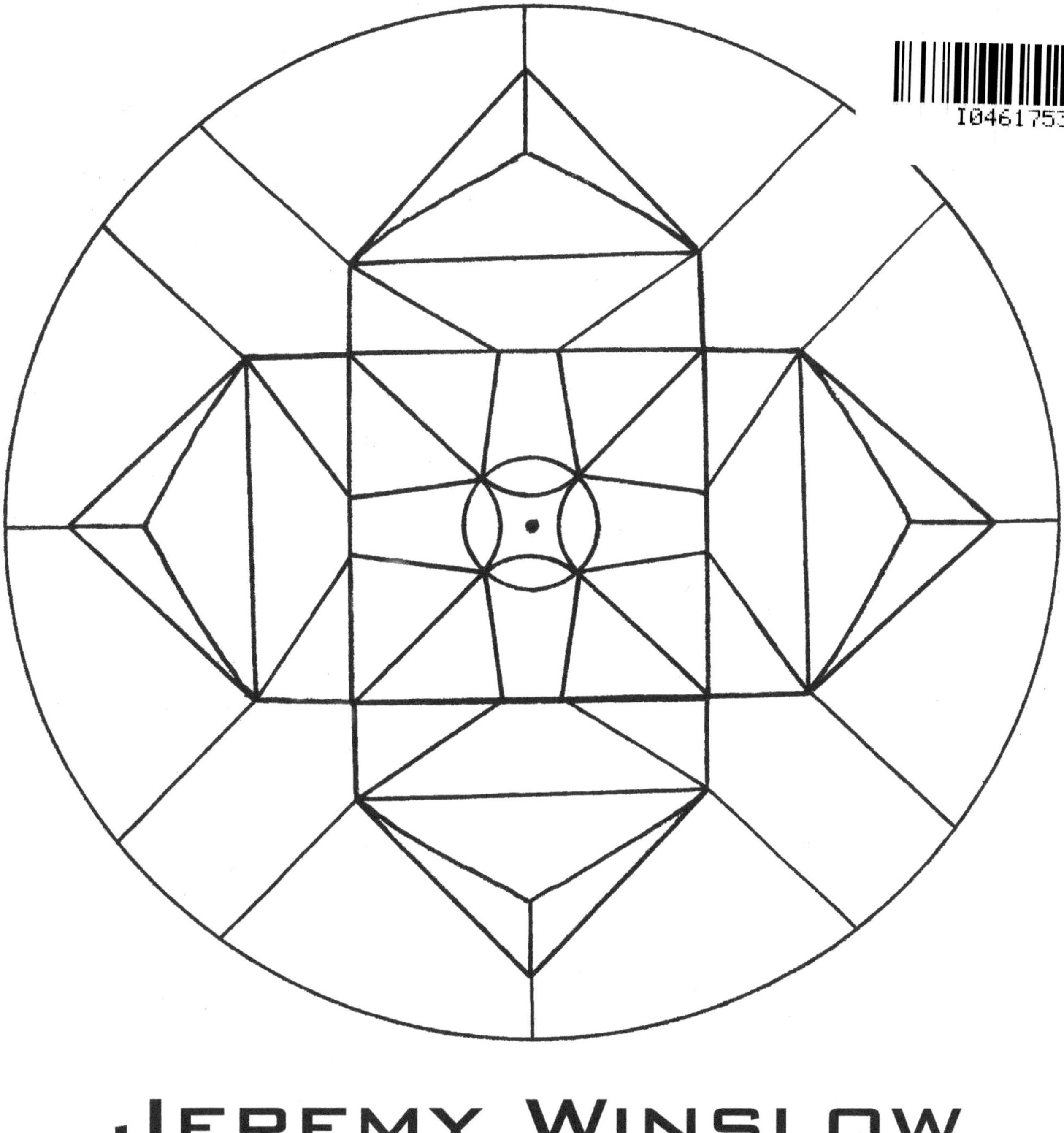

I0461753

JEREMY WINSLOW

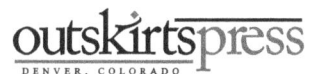
DENVER, COLORADO

Coloring Fun with Geometric Designs
Volume 1
All Rights Reserved.
Copyright © 2015 Jeremy Winslow
v1.0

Outskirts Press, Inc.
http://www.outskirtspress.com

ISBN: 978-1-4787-6368-0

Outskirts Press and the "OP" logo are trademarks belonging to Outskirts Press, Inc.

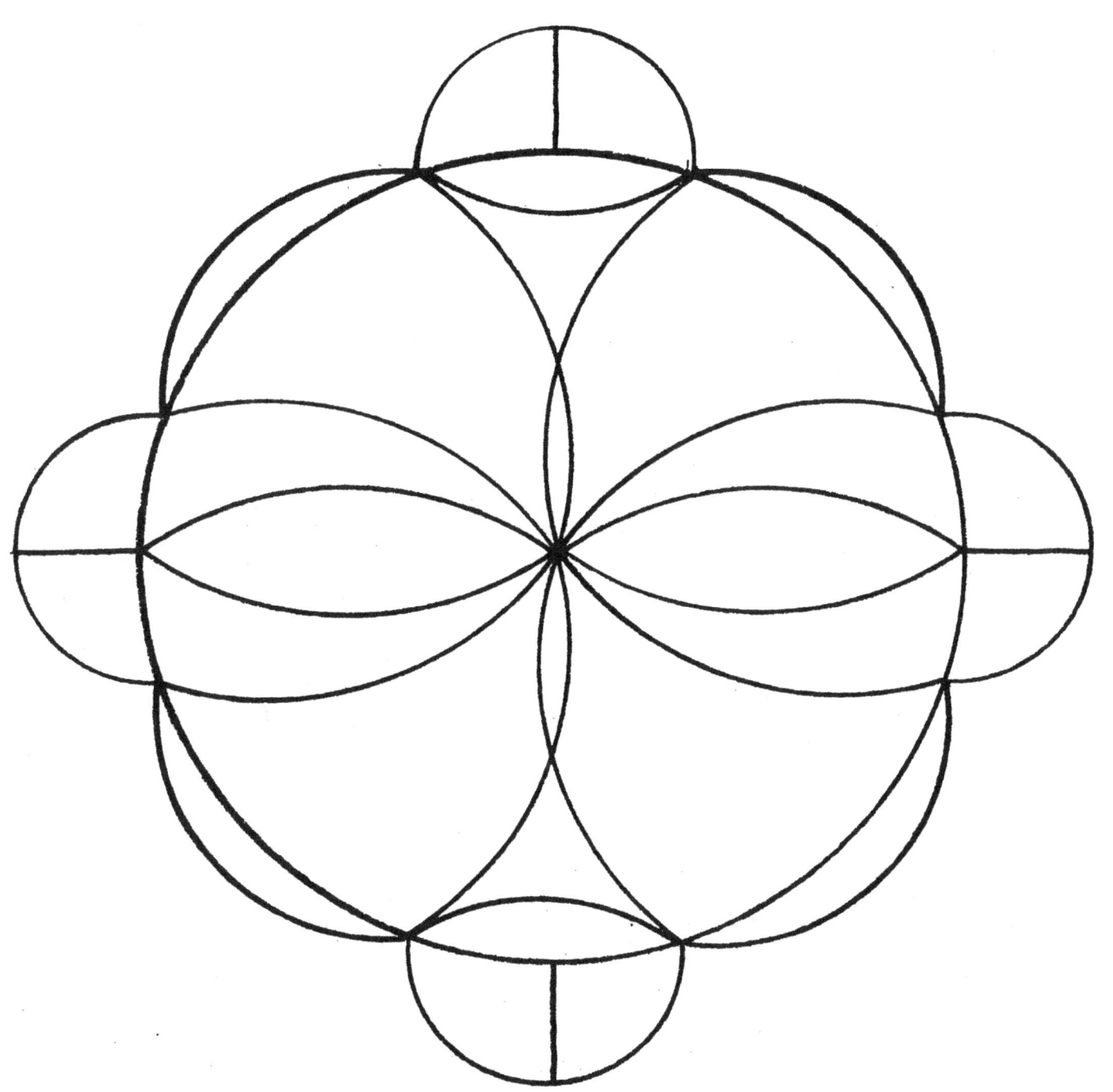

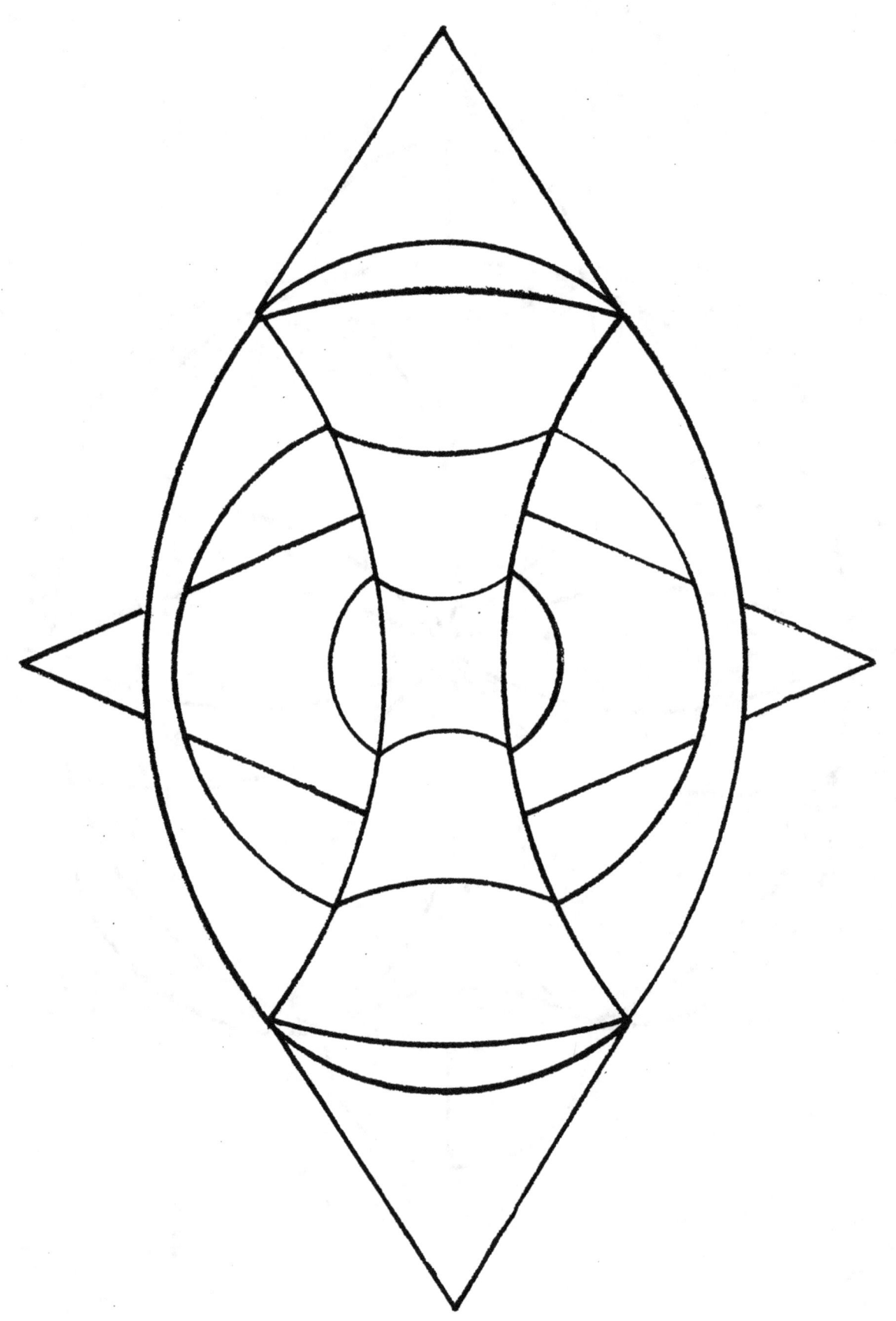

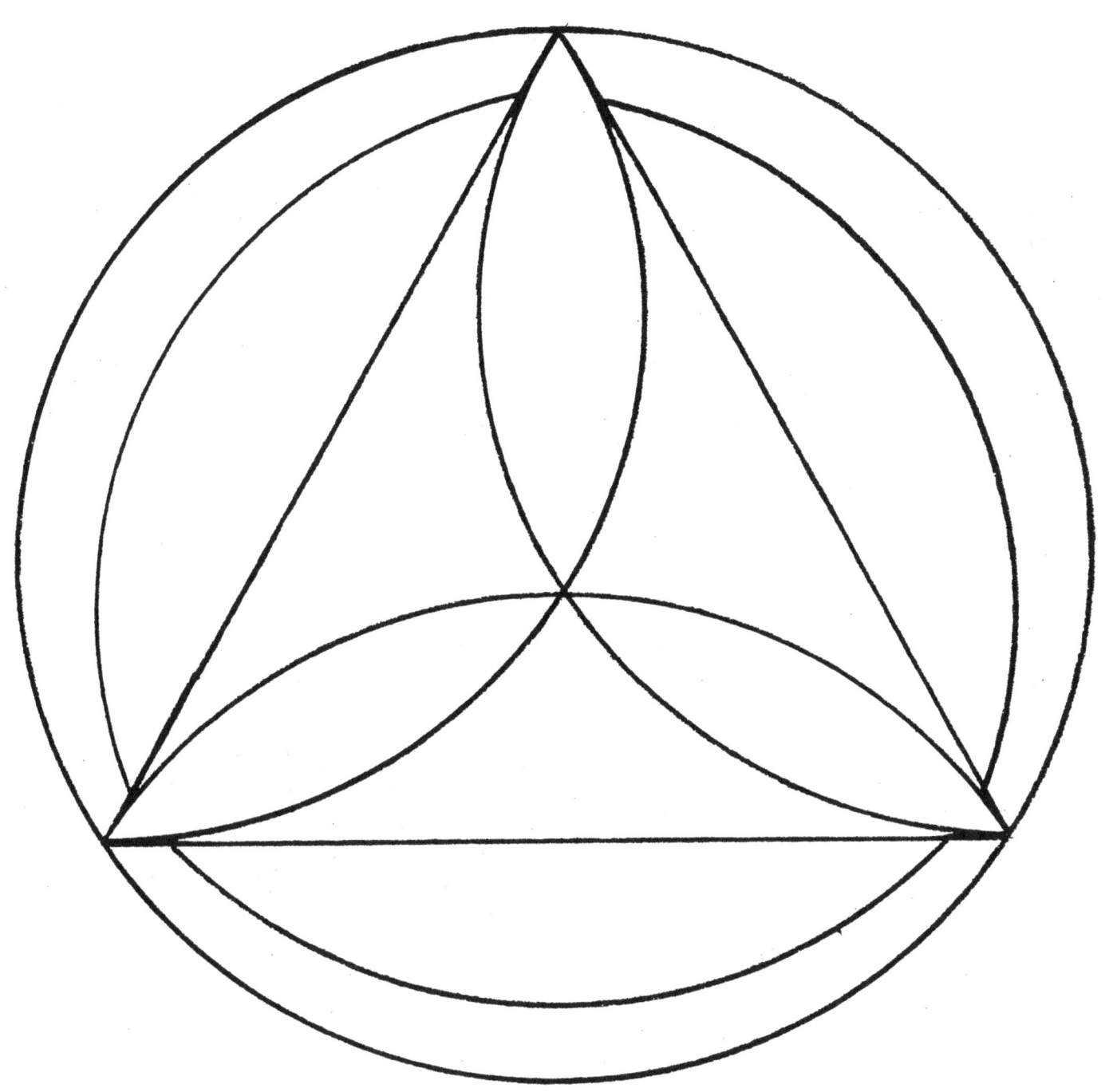

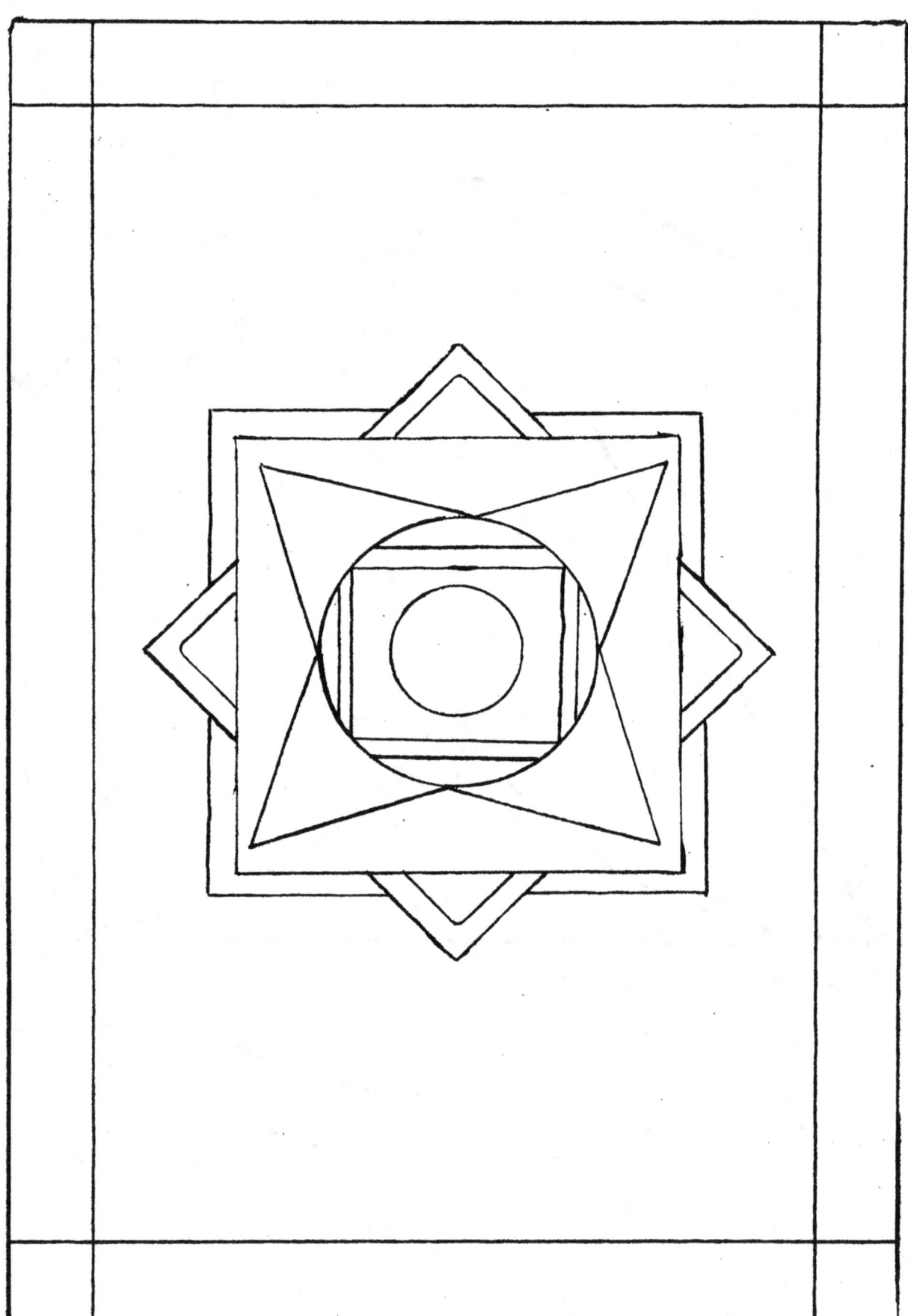

4

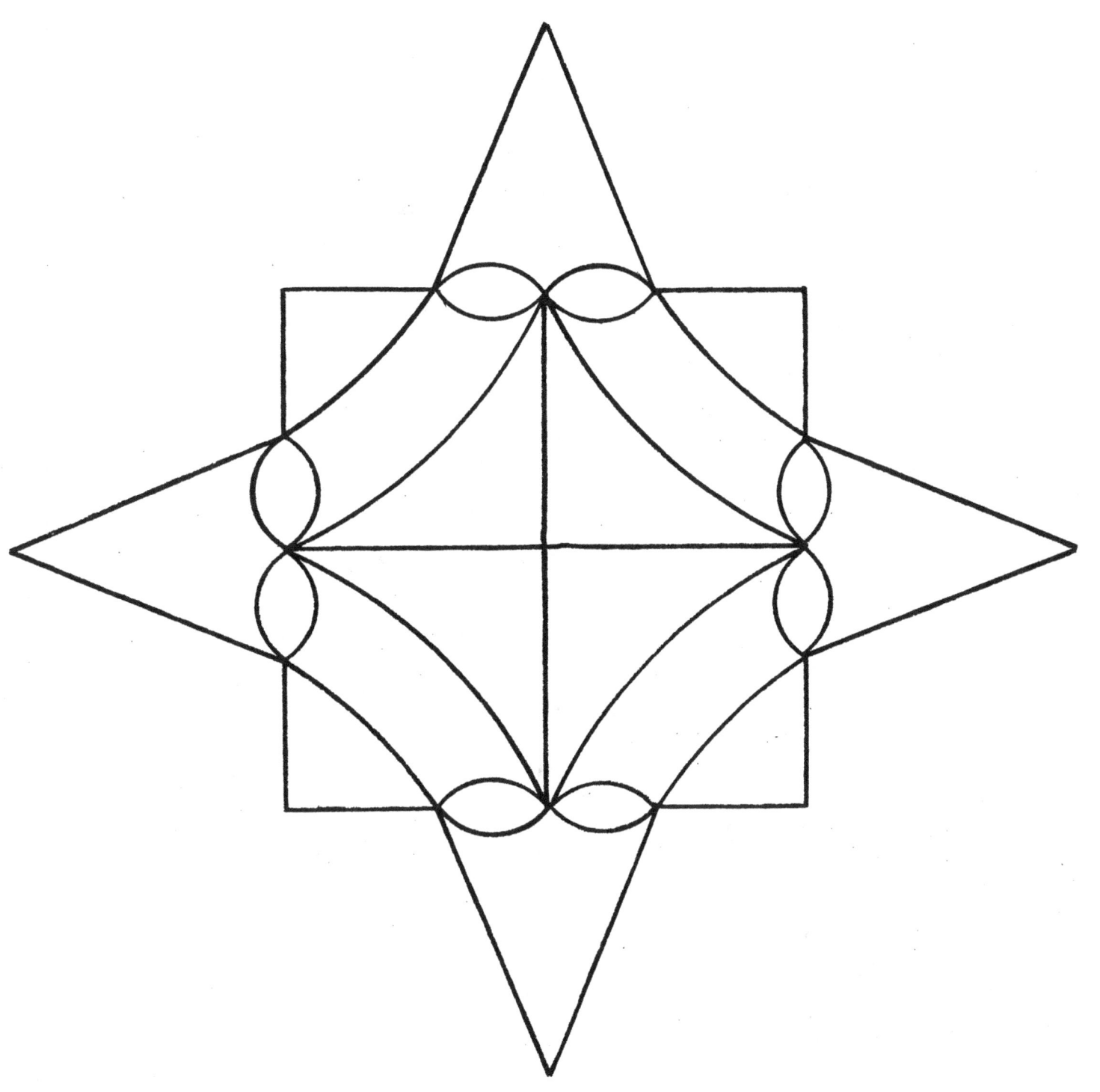

5

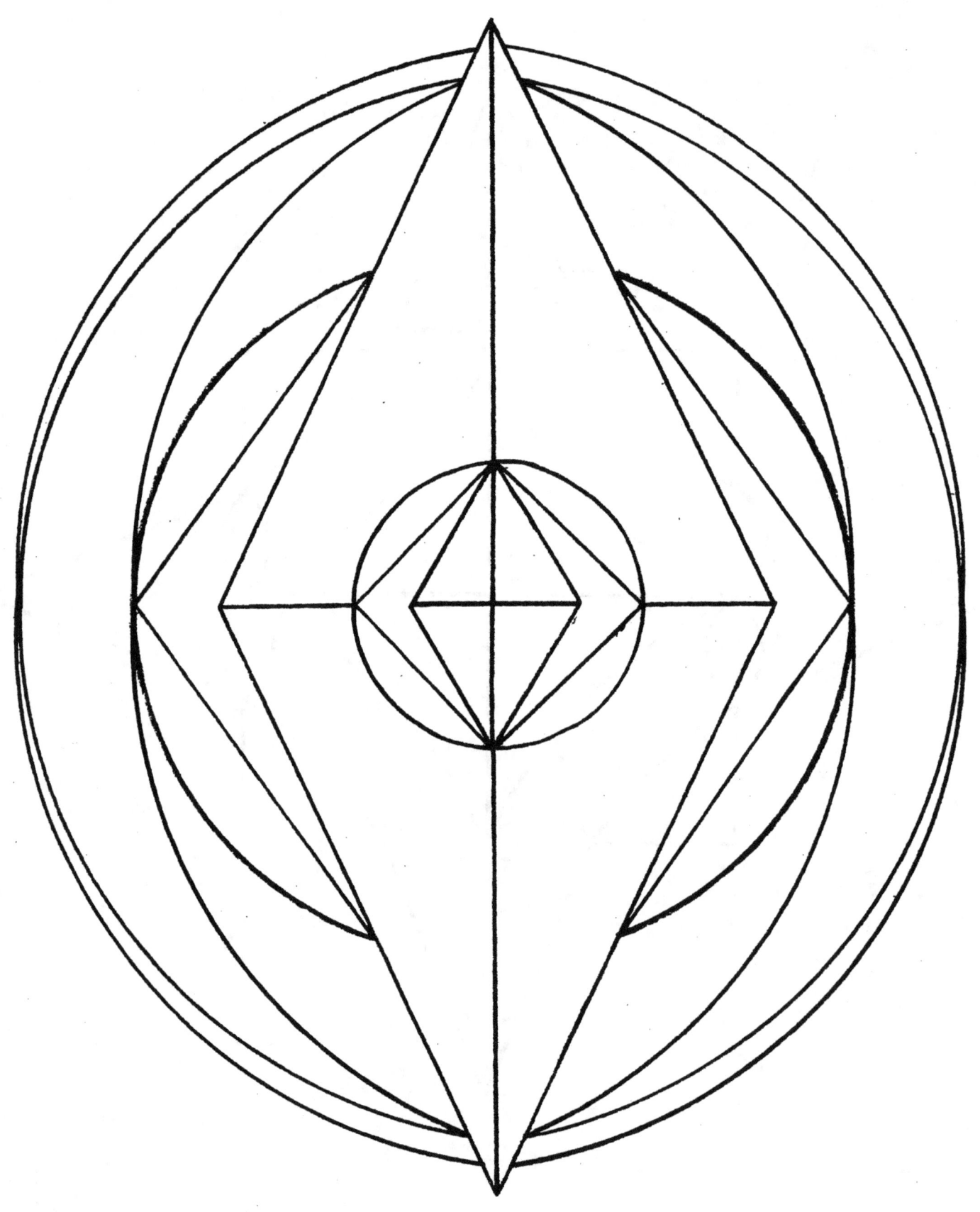

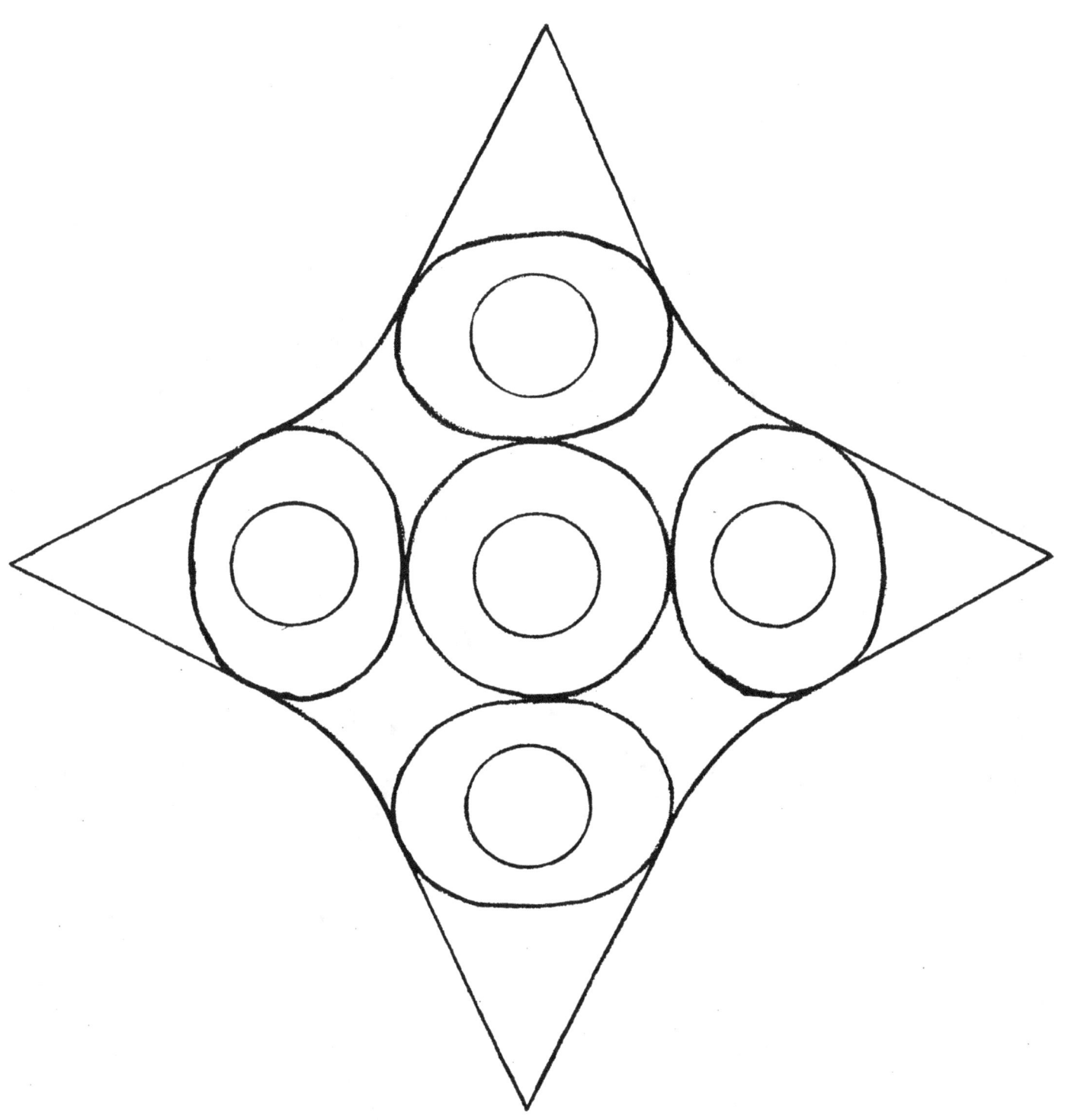

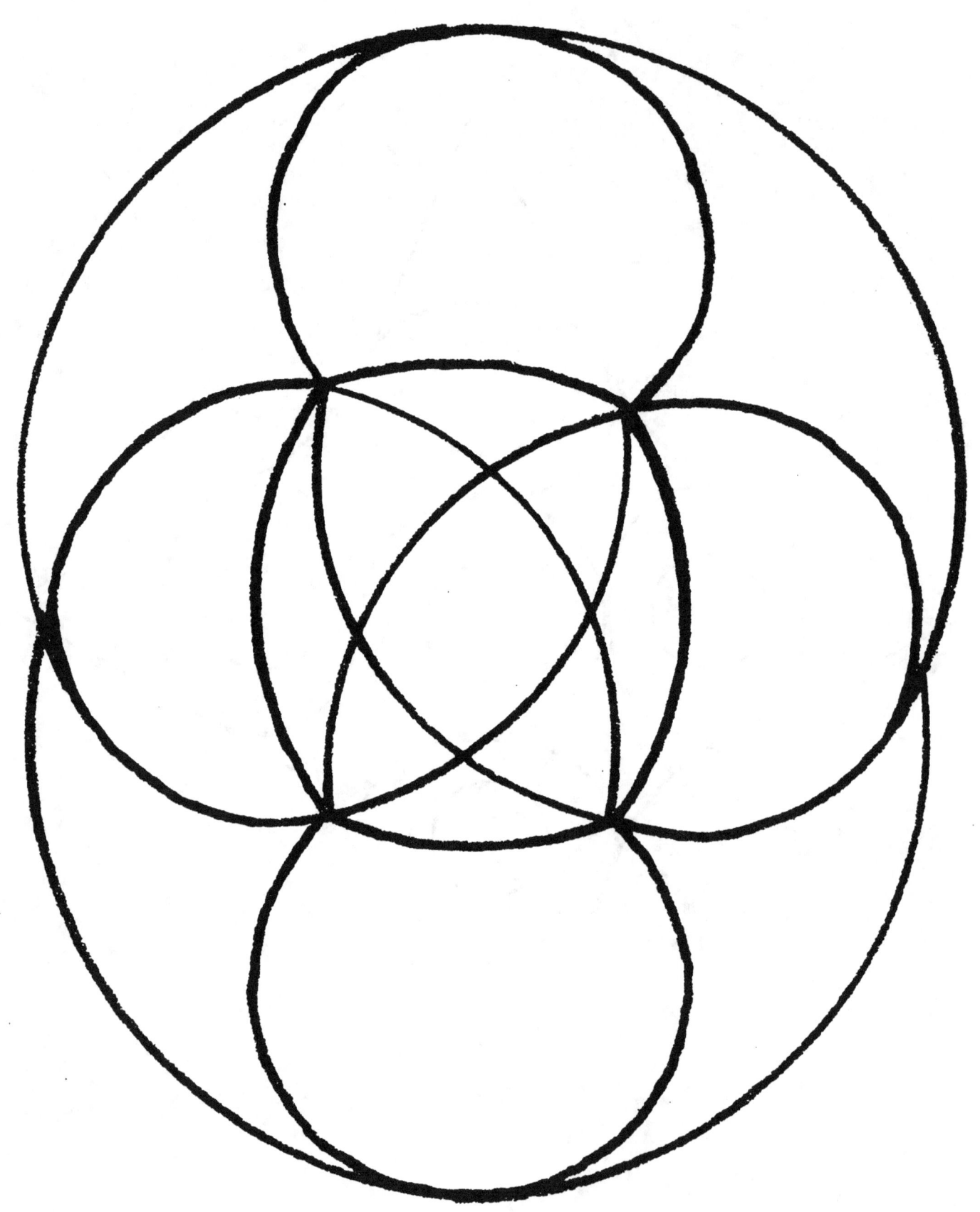

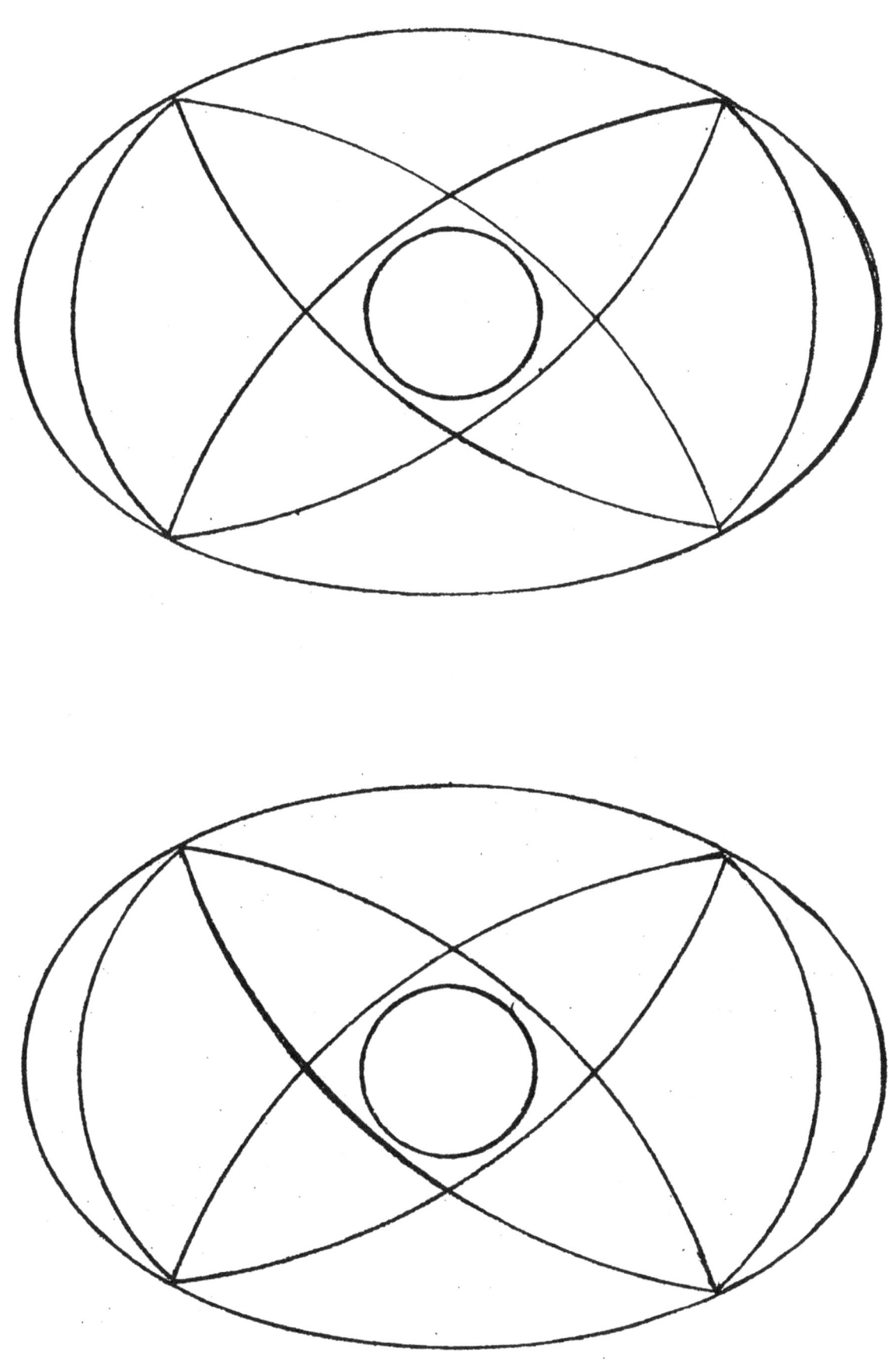

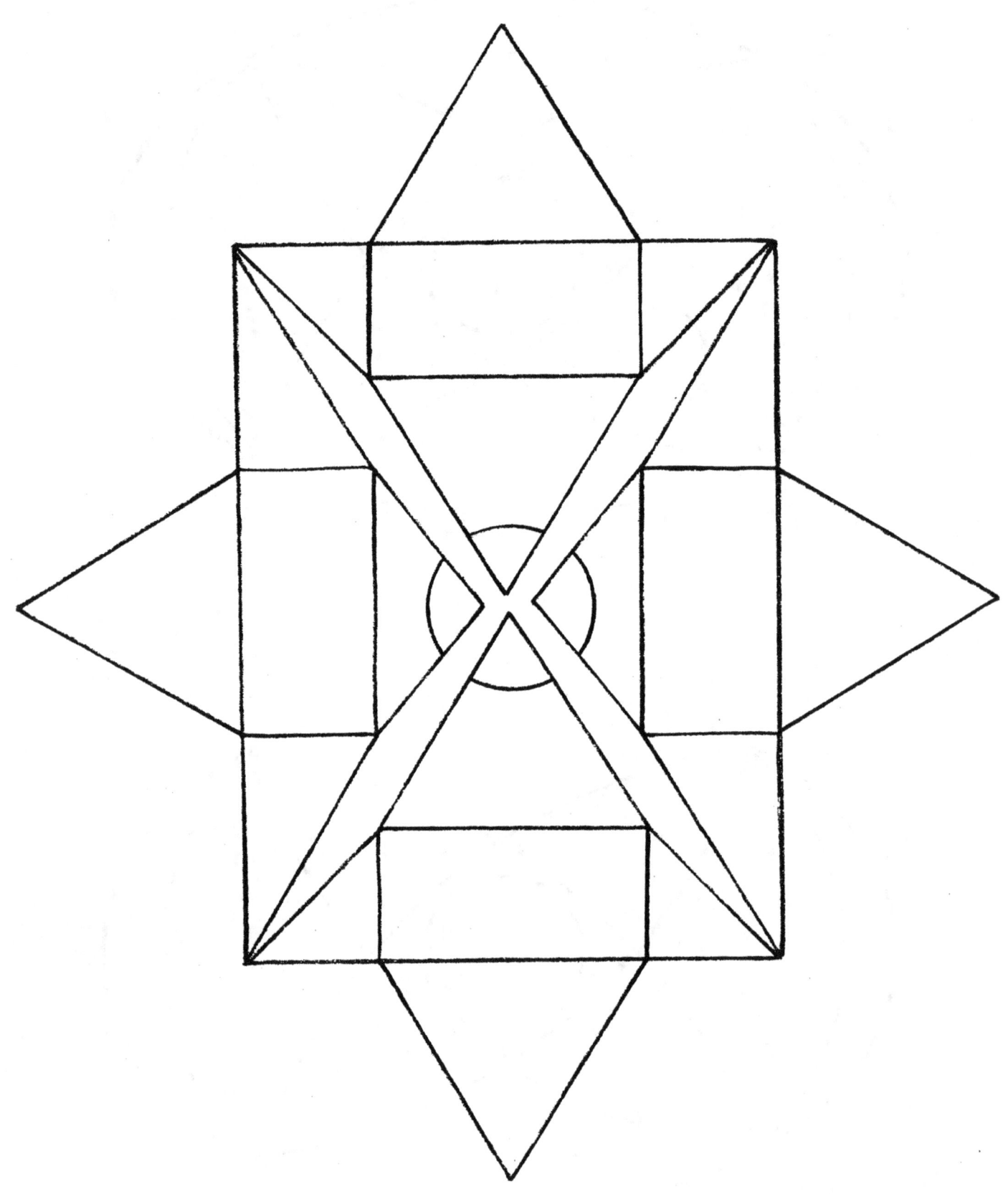

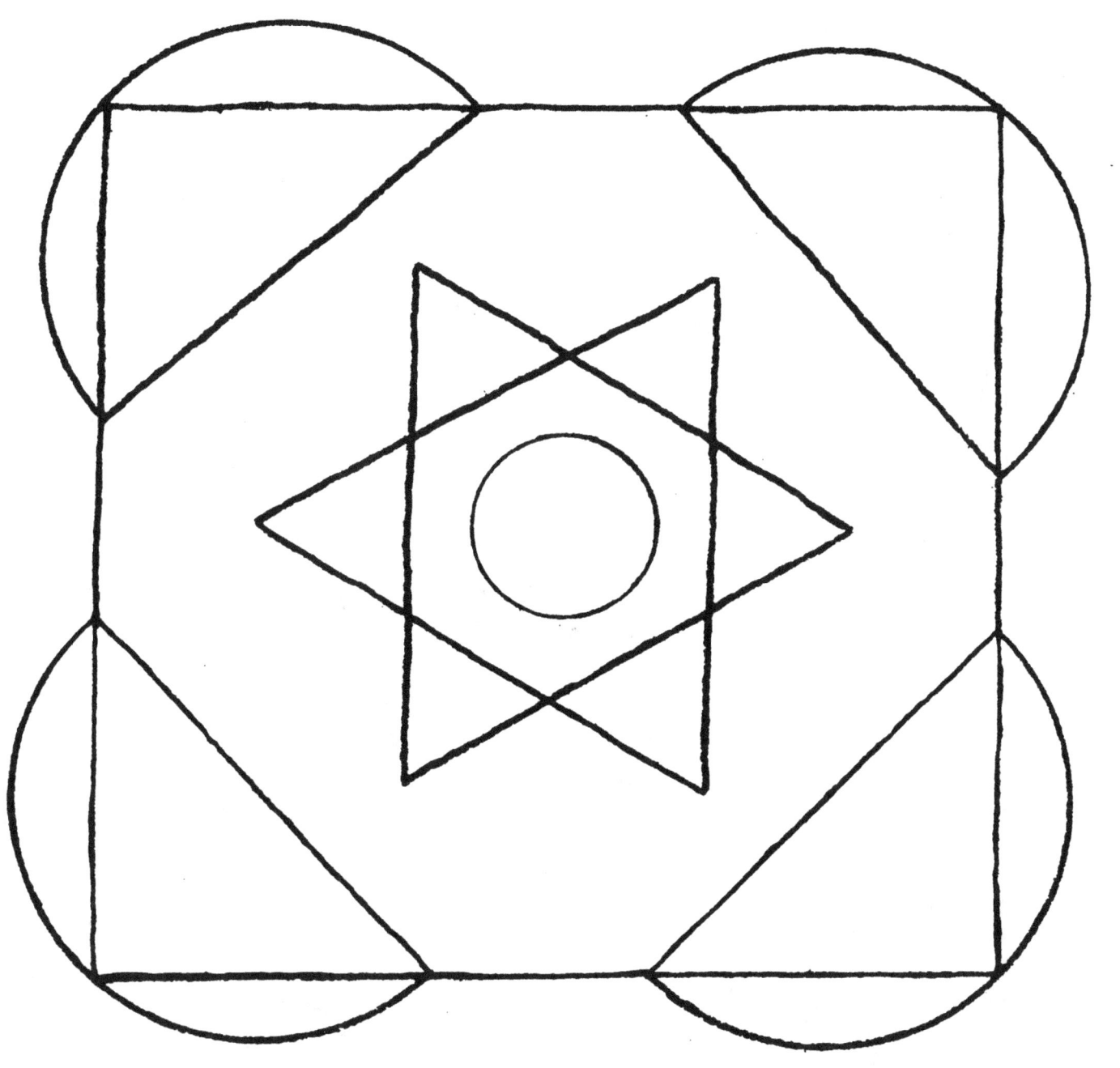

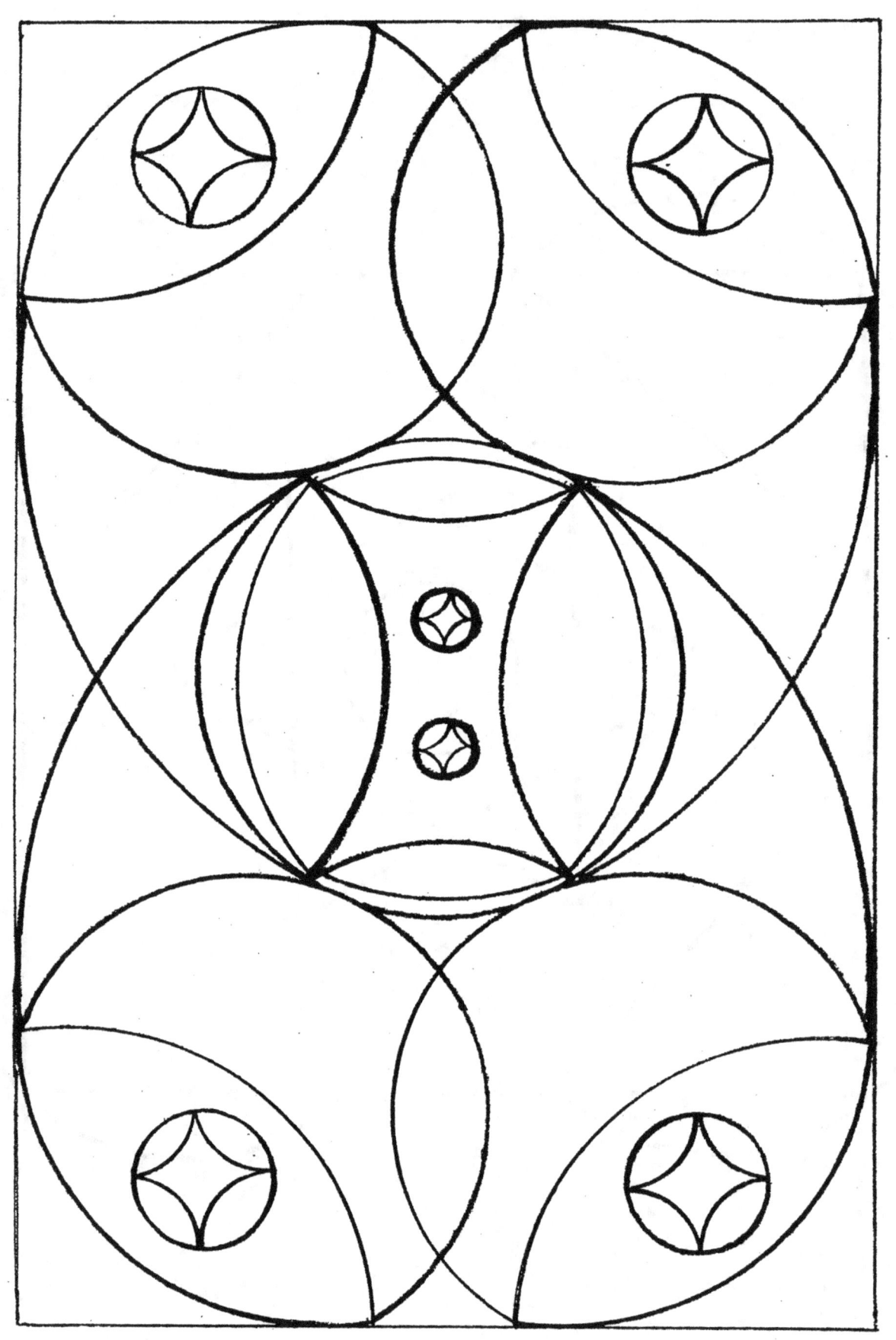

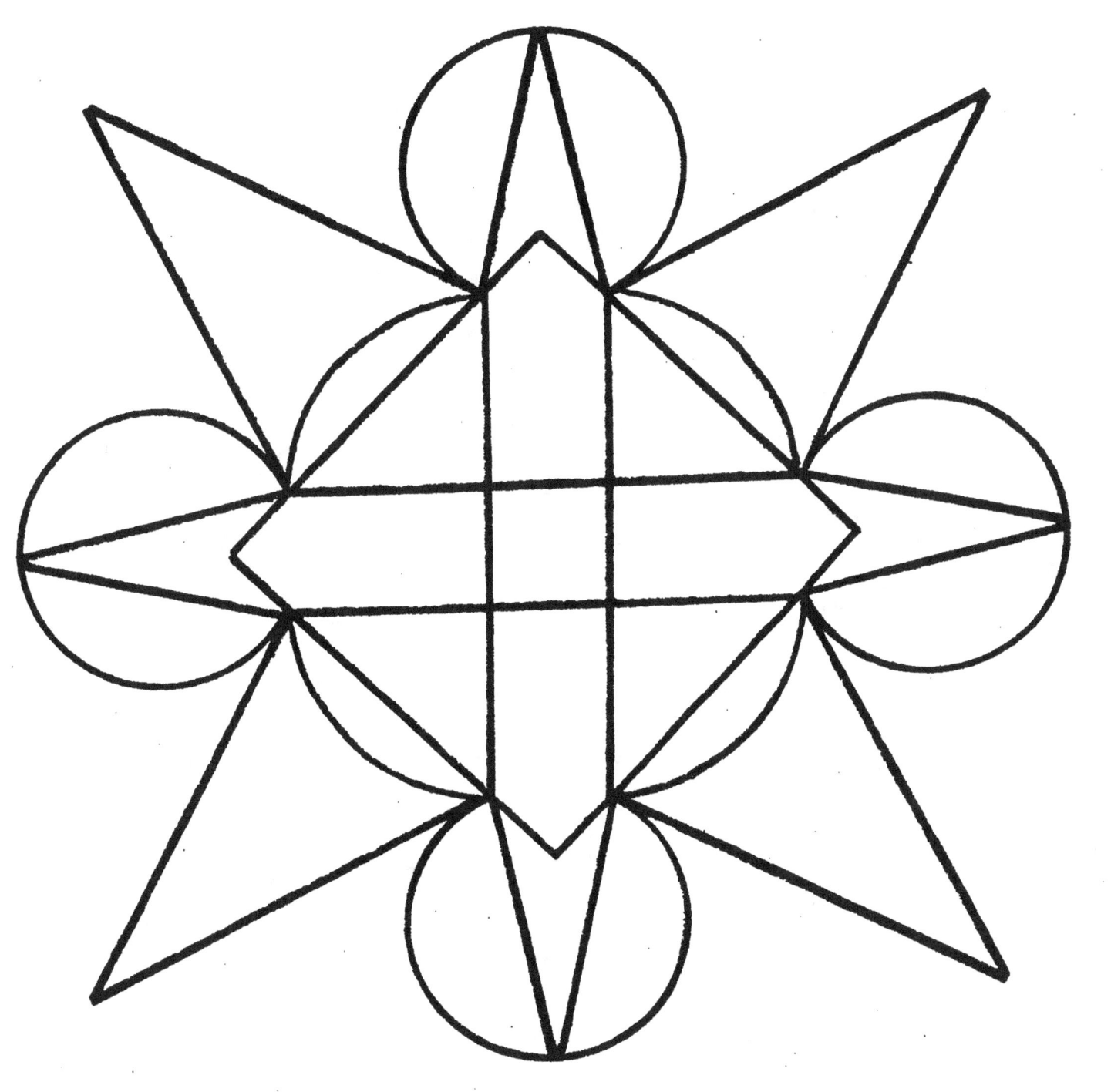

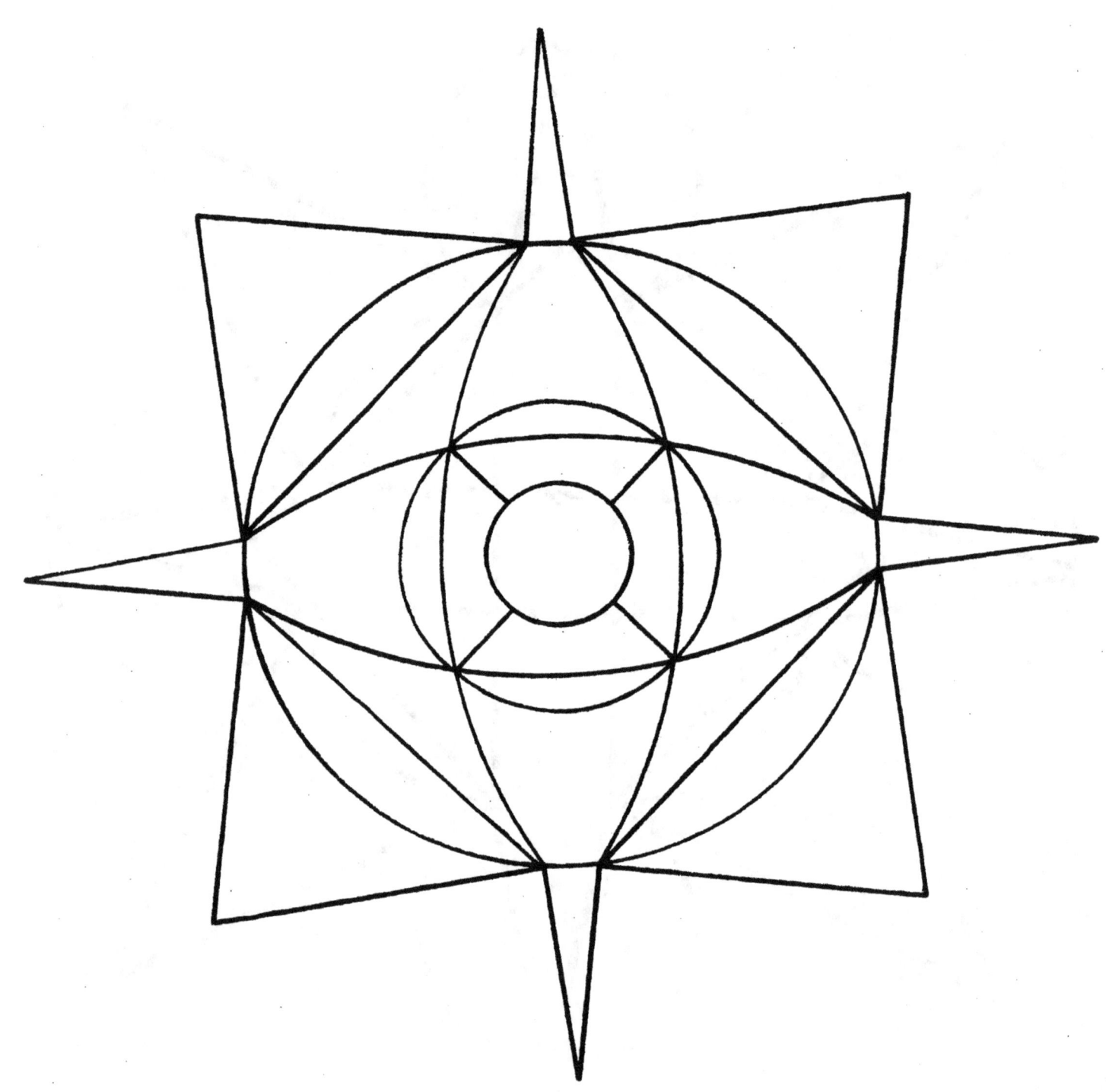

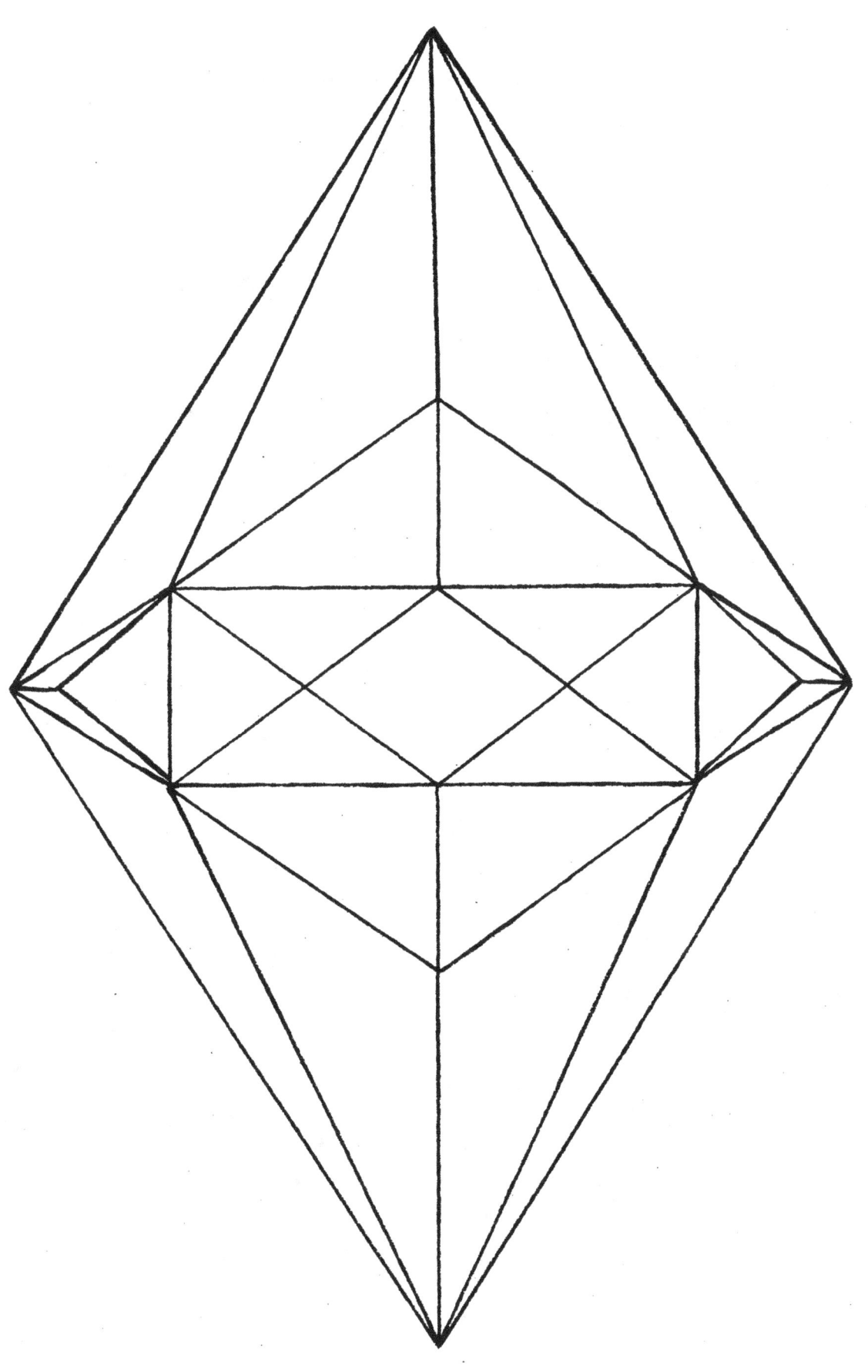

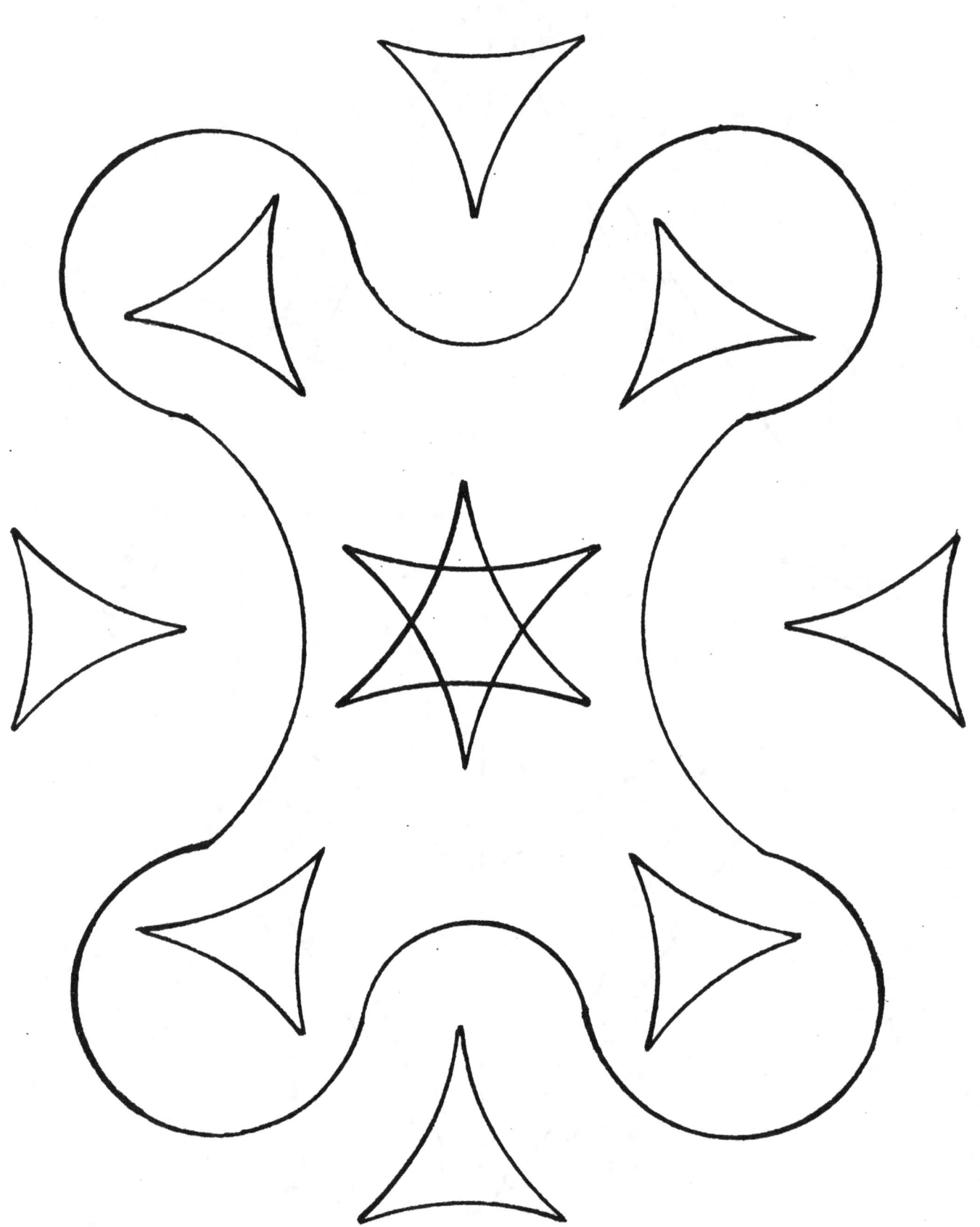

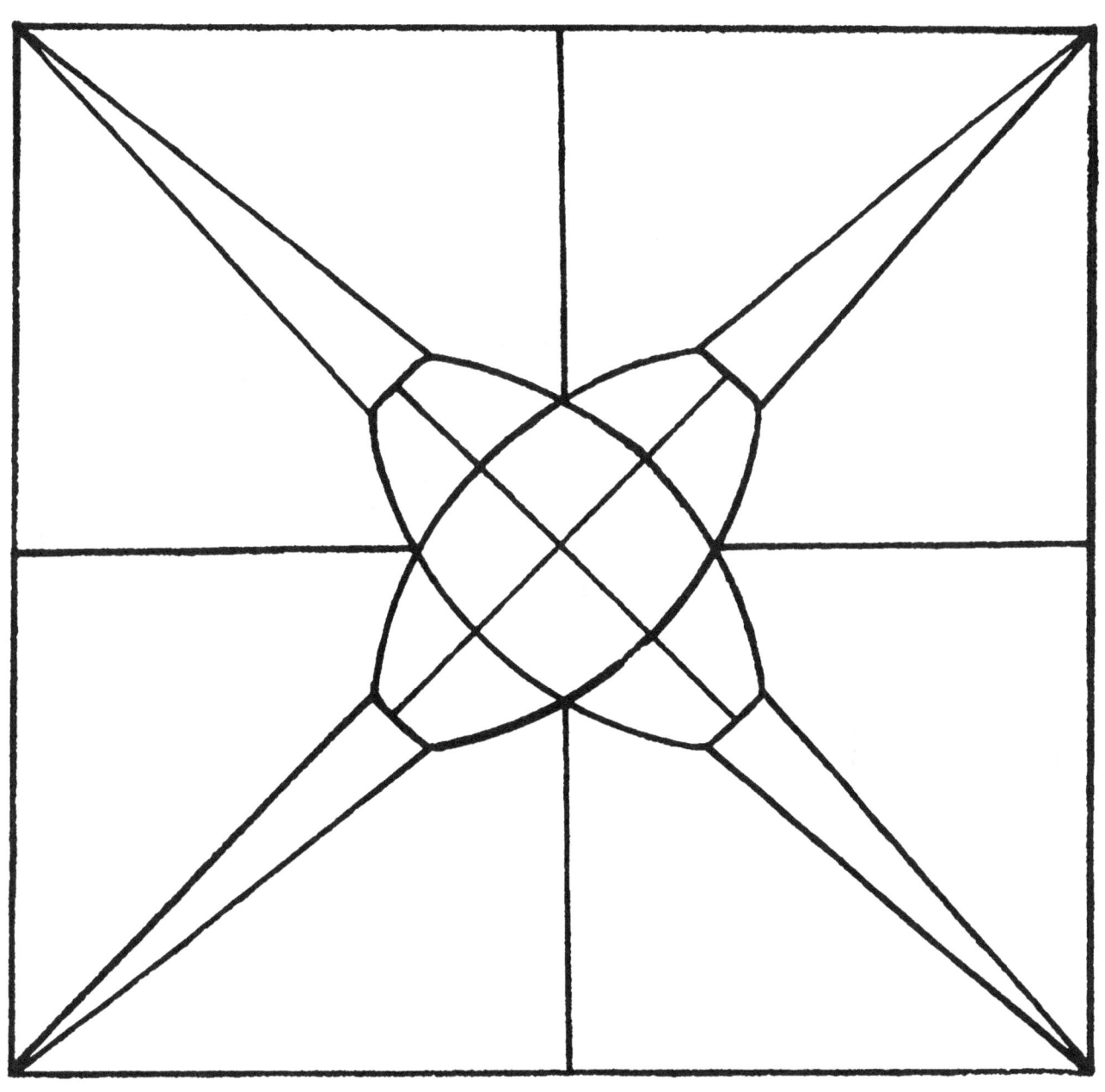

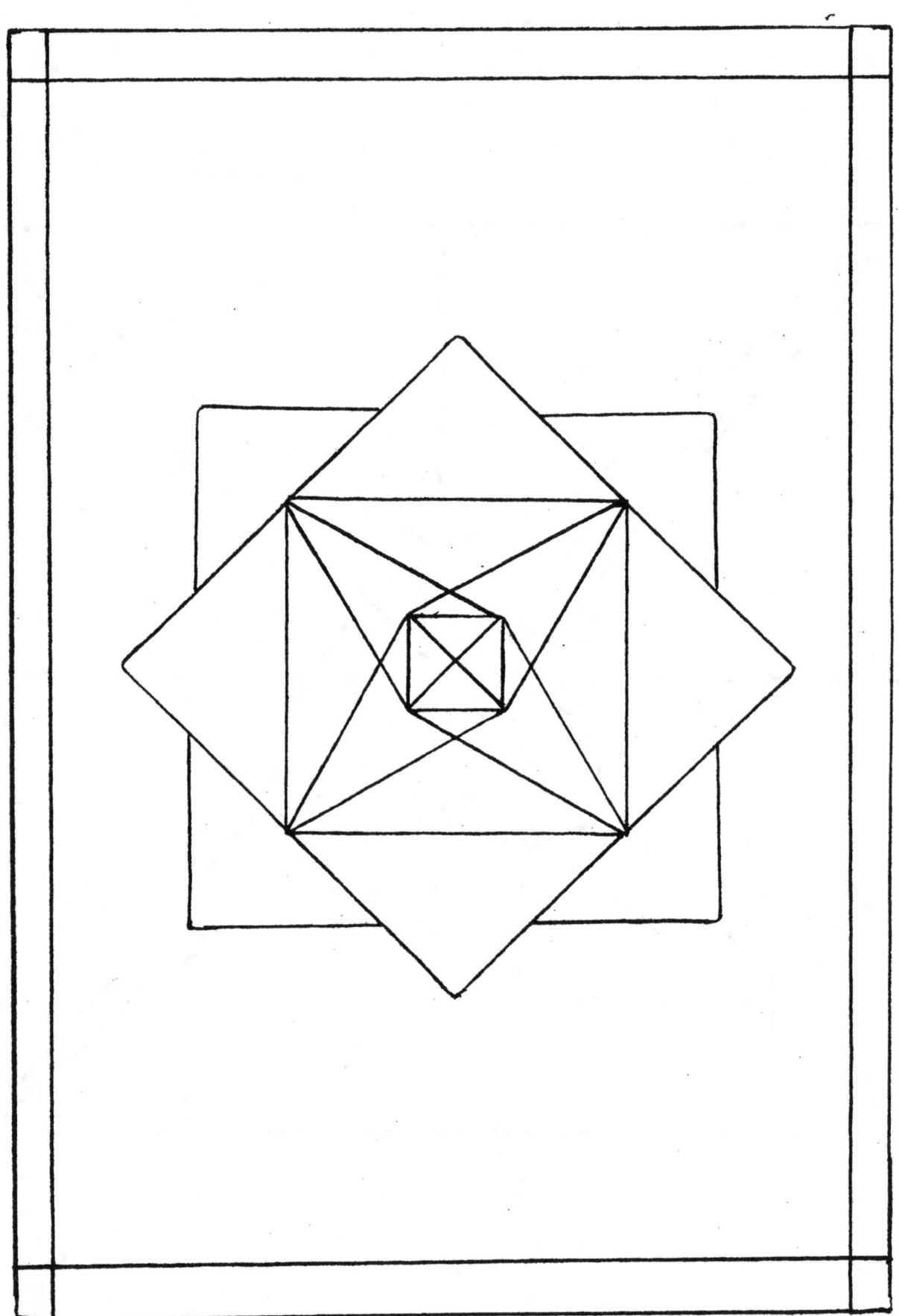

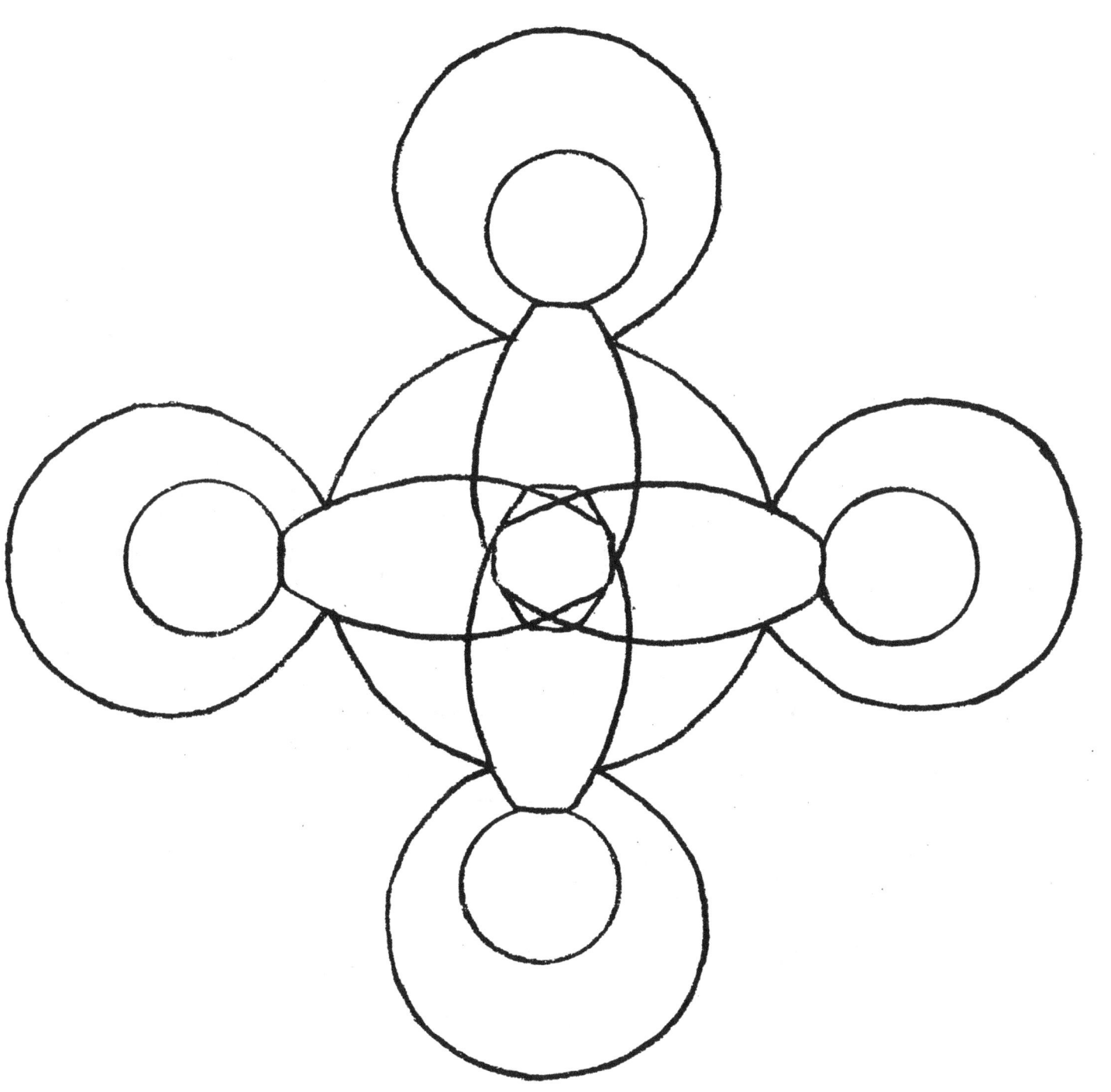

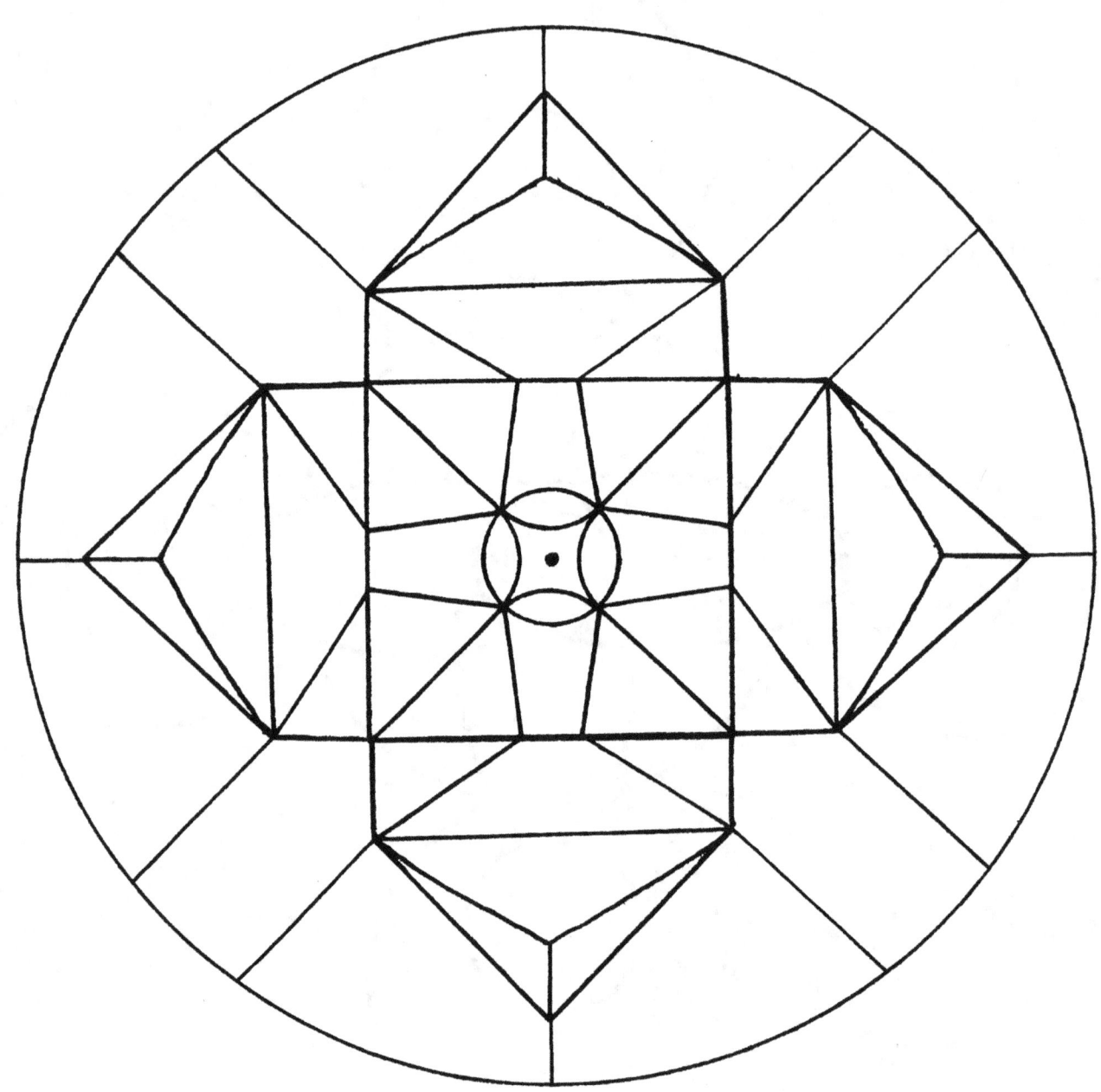

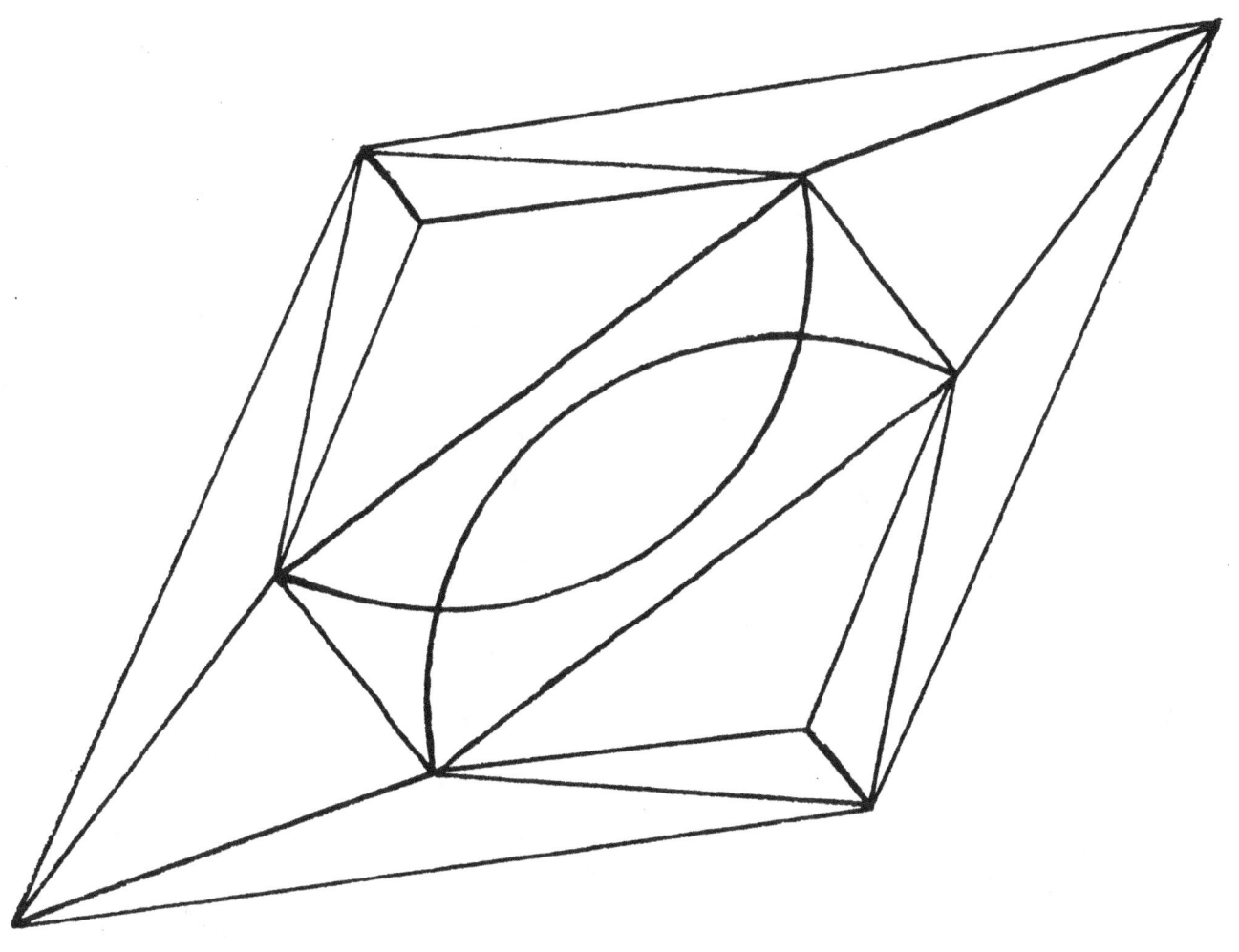

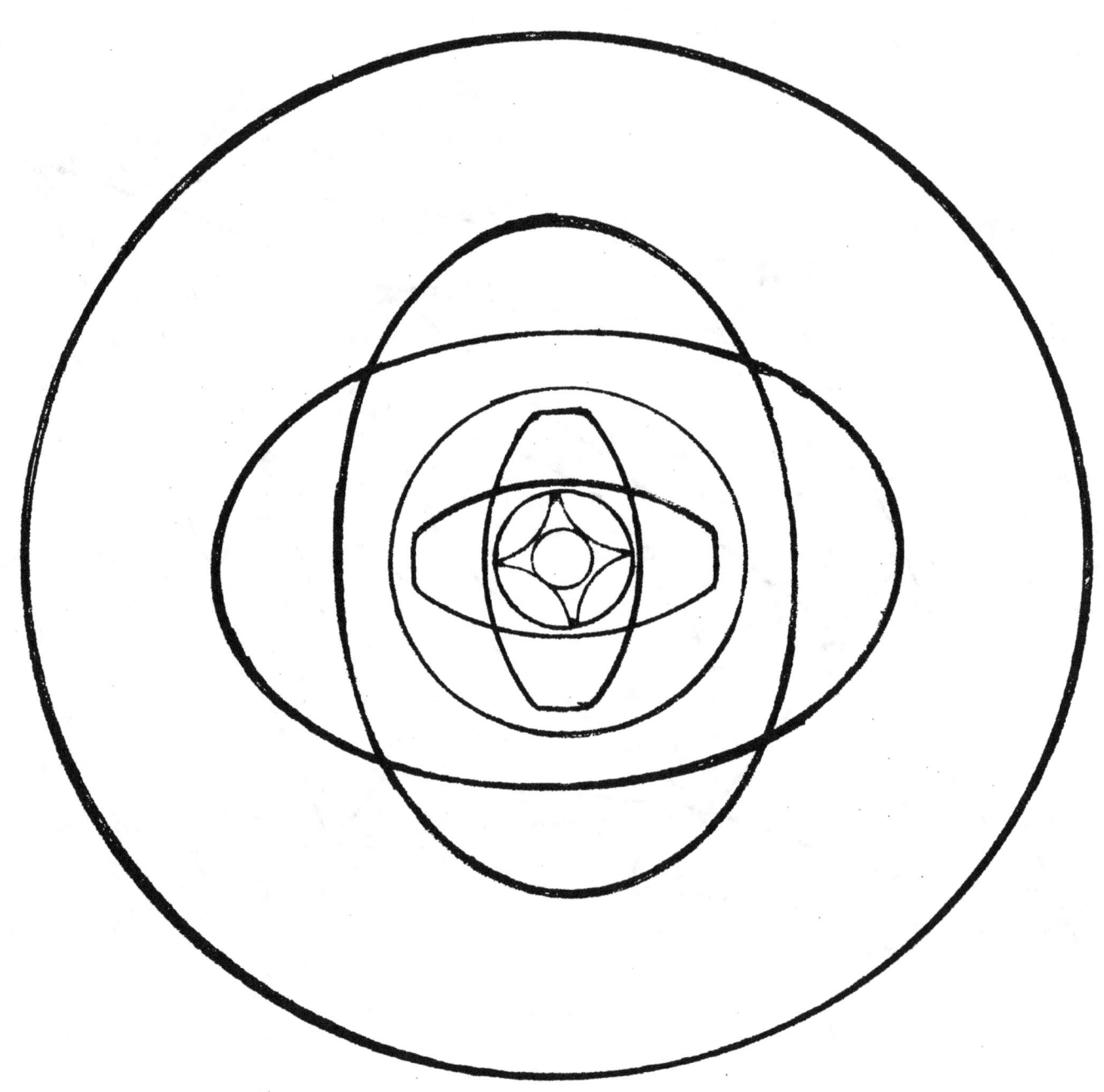

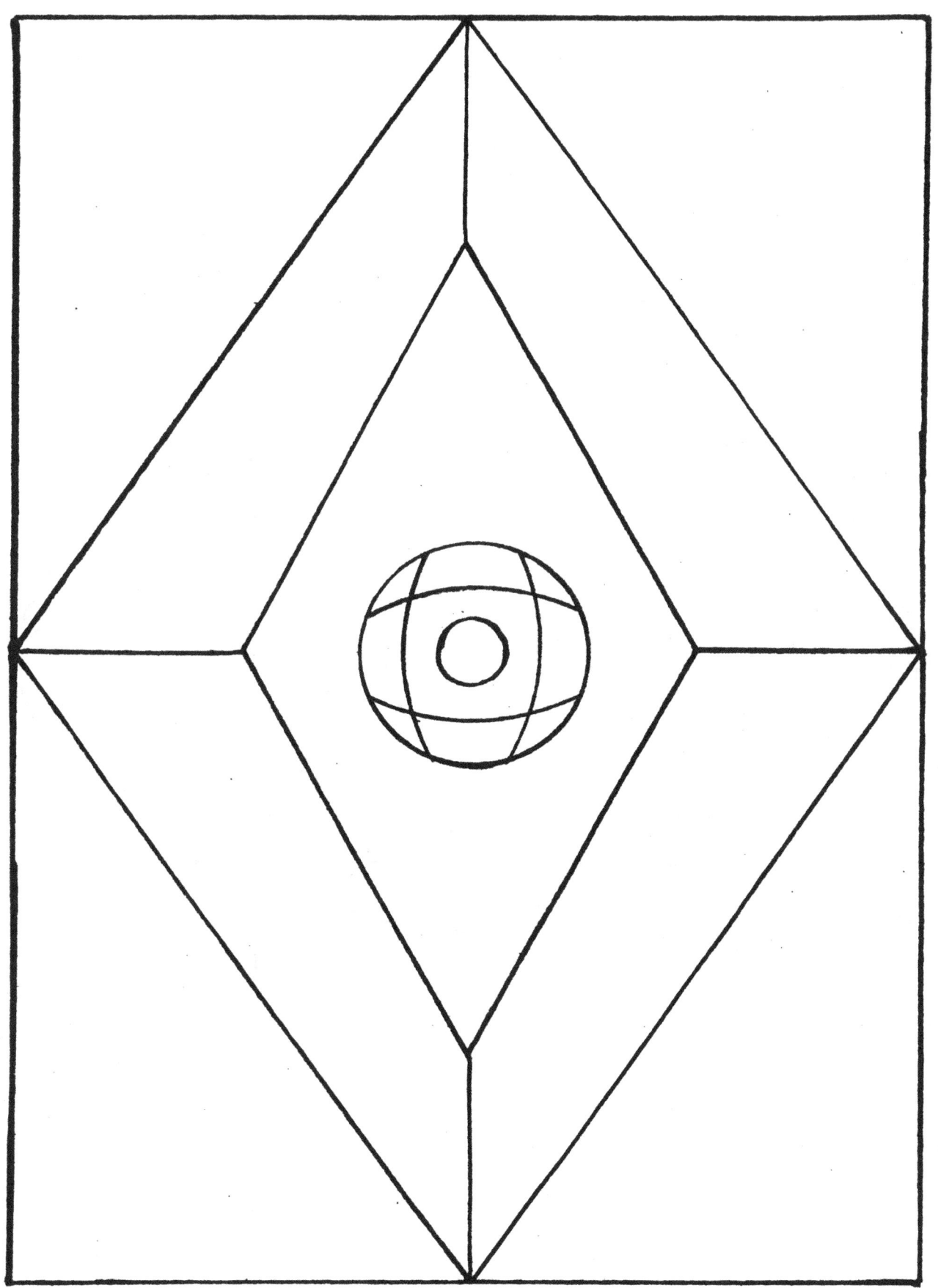

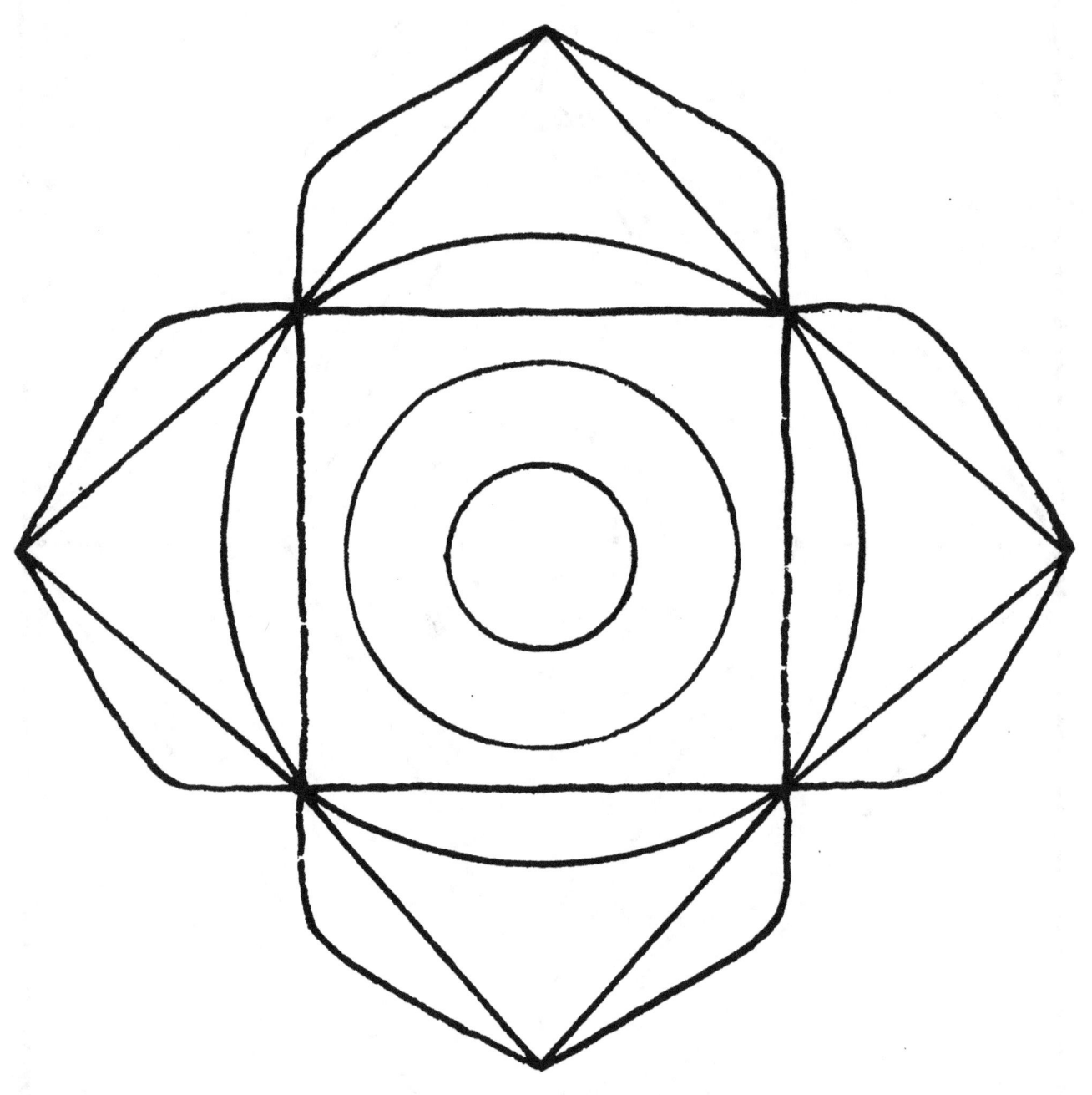

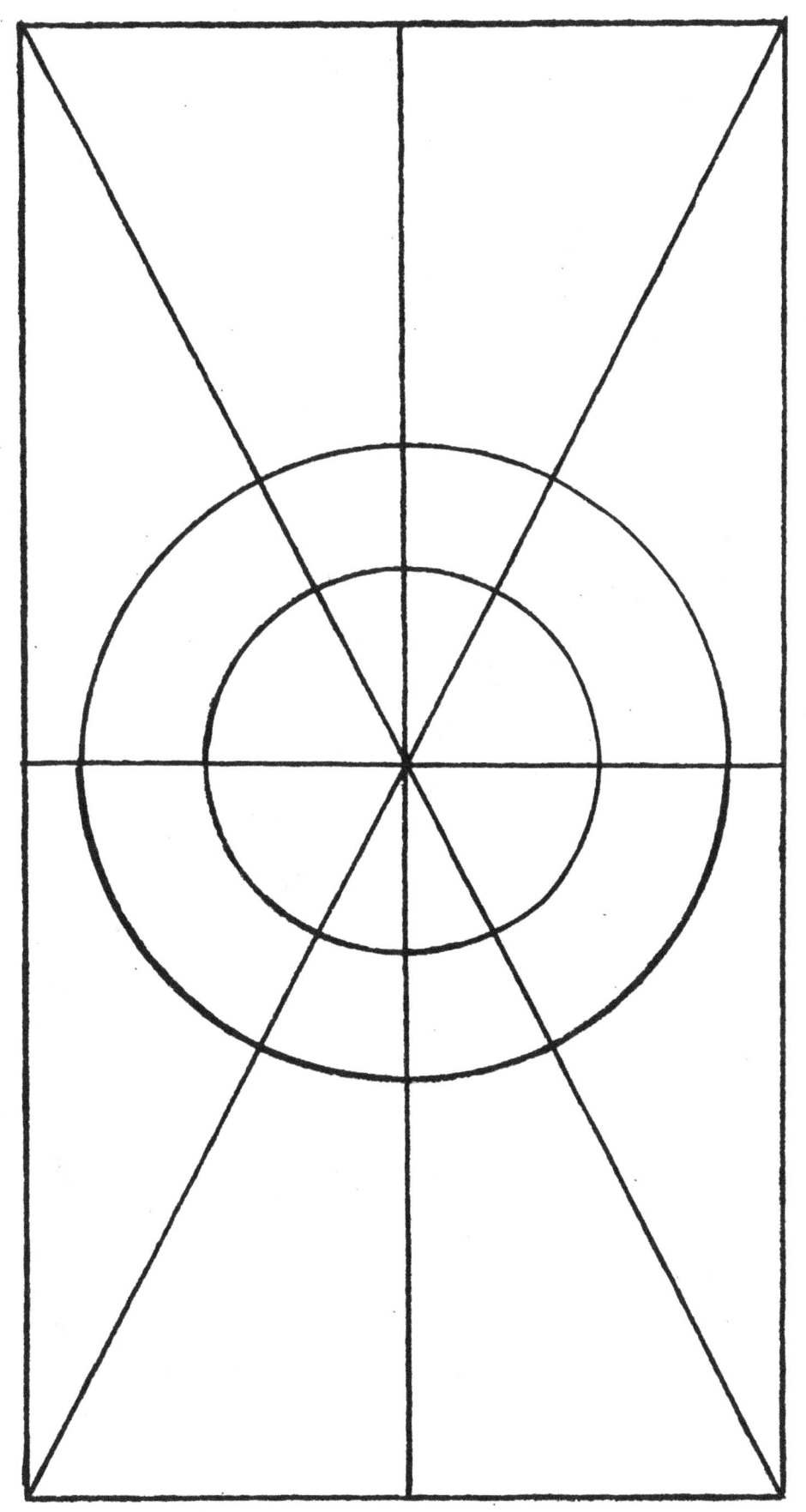

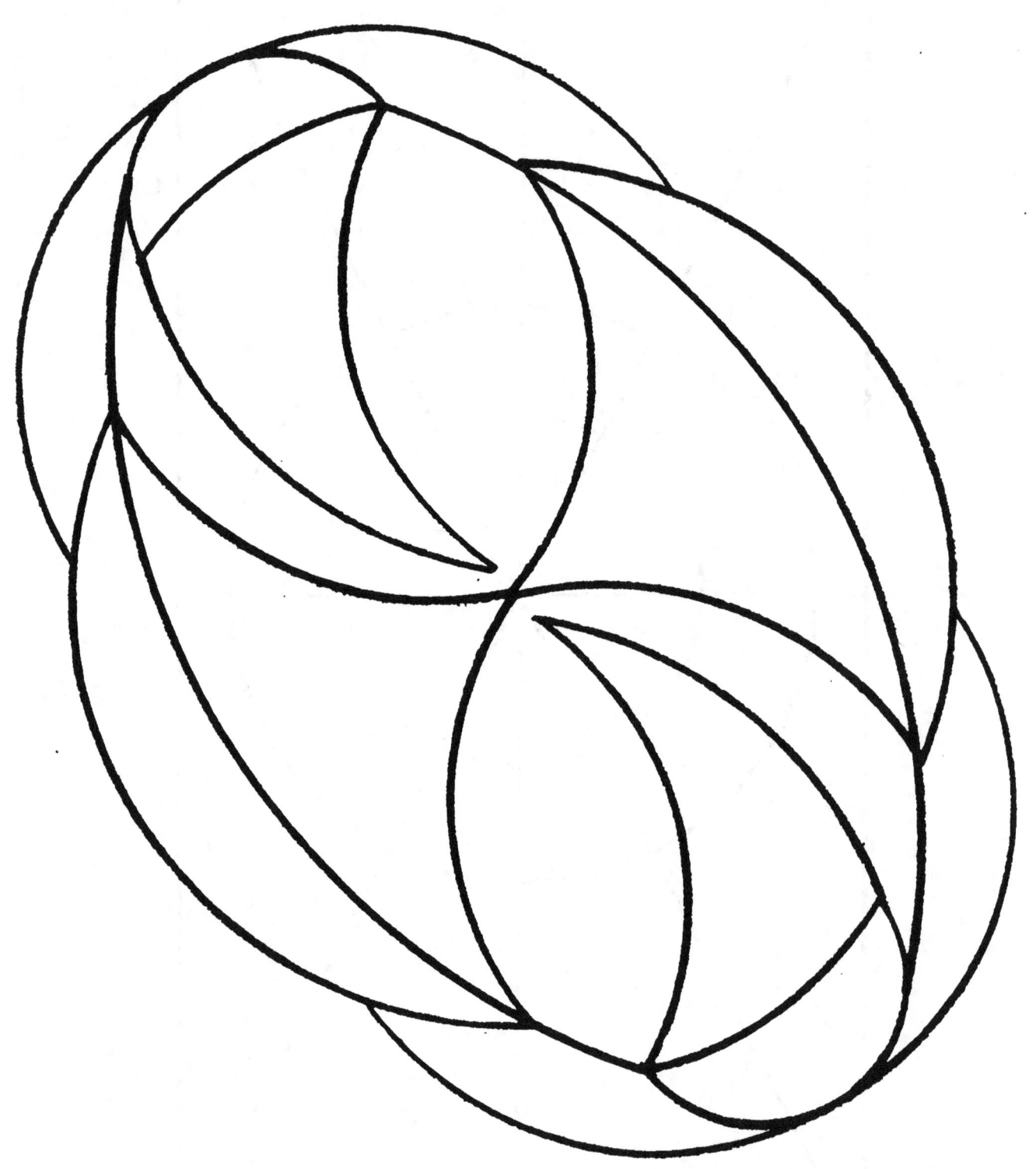

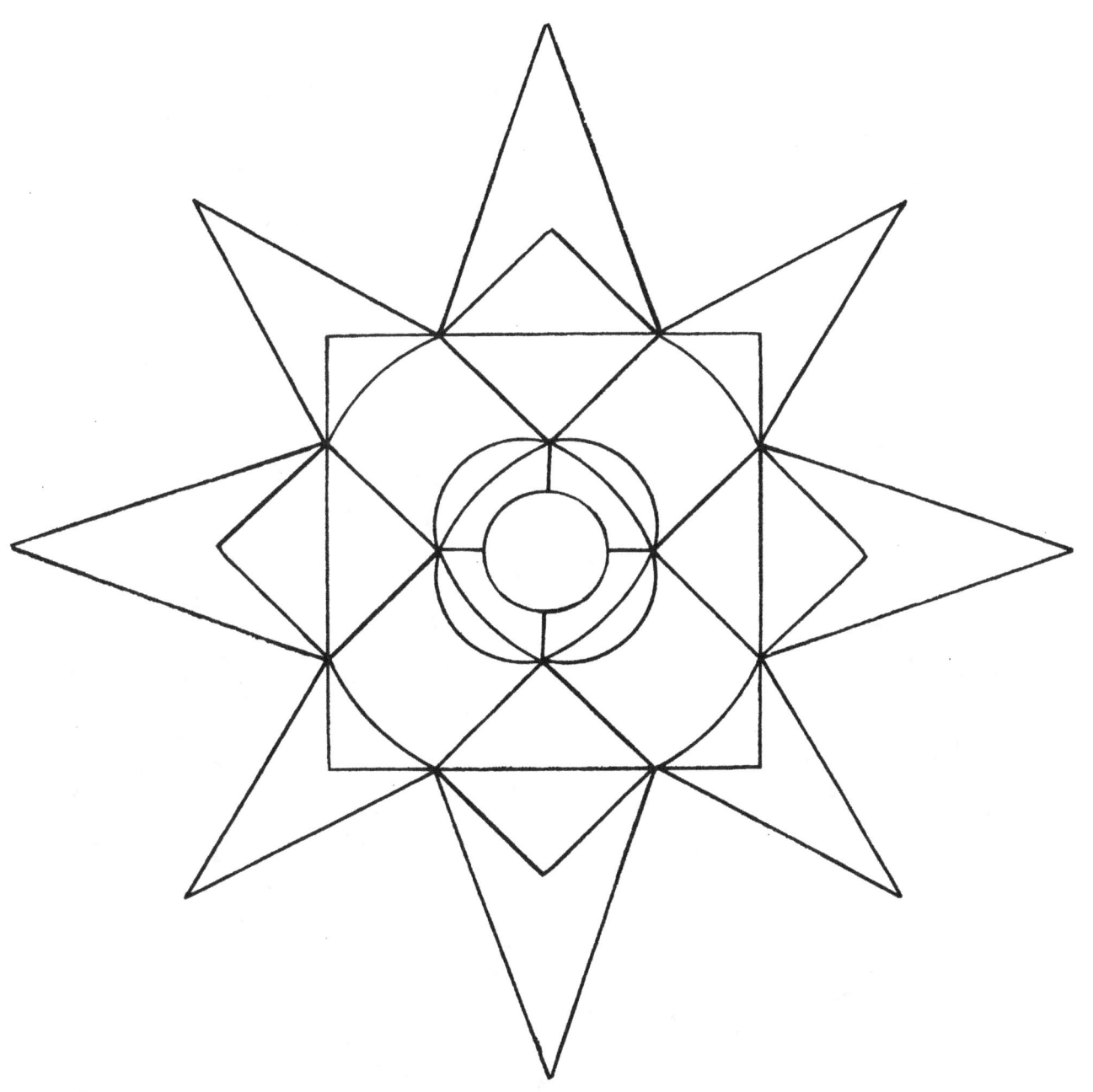

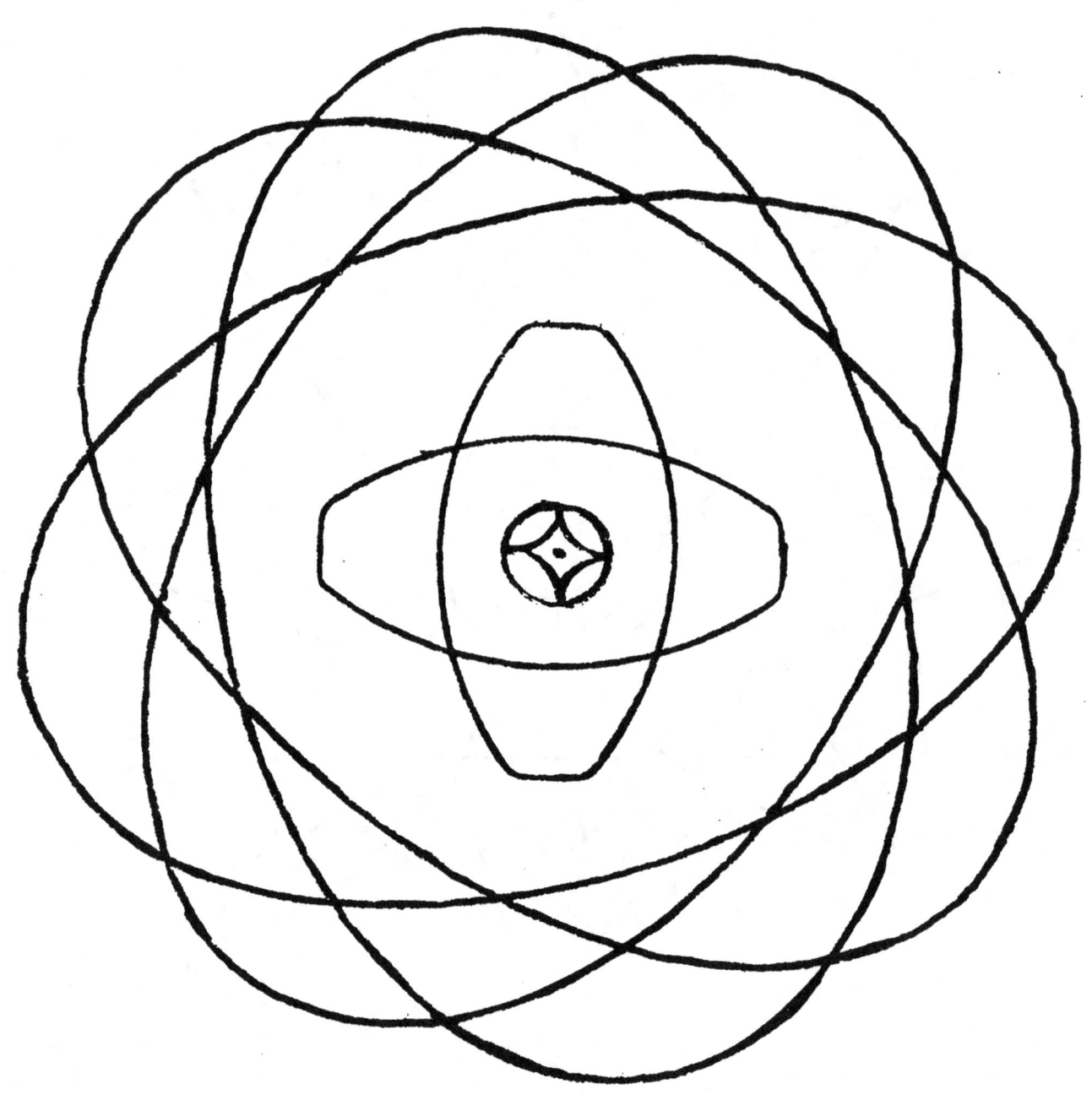

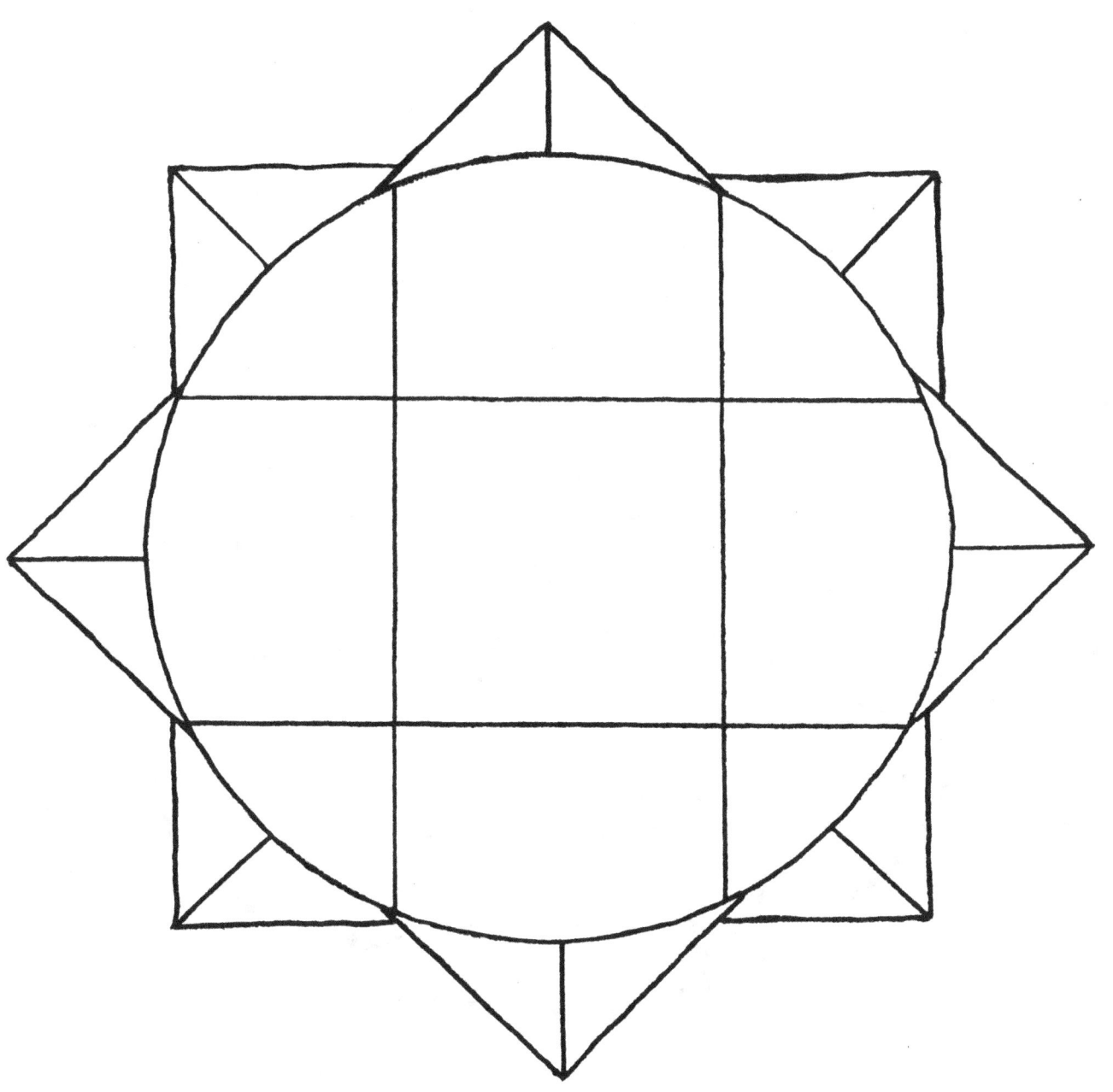

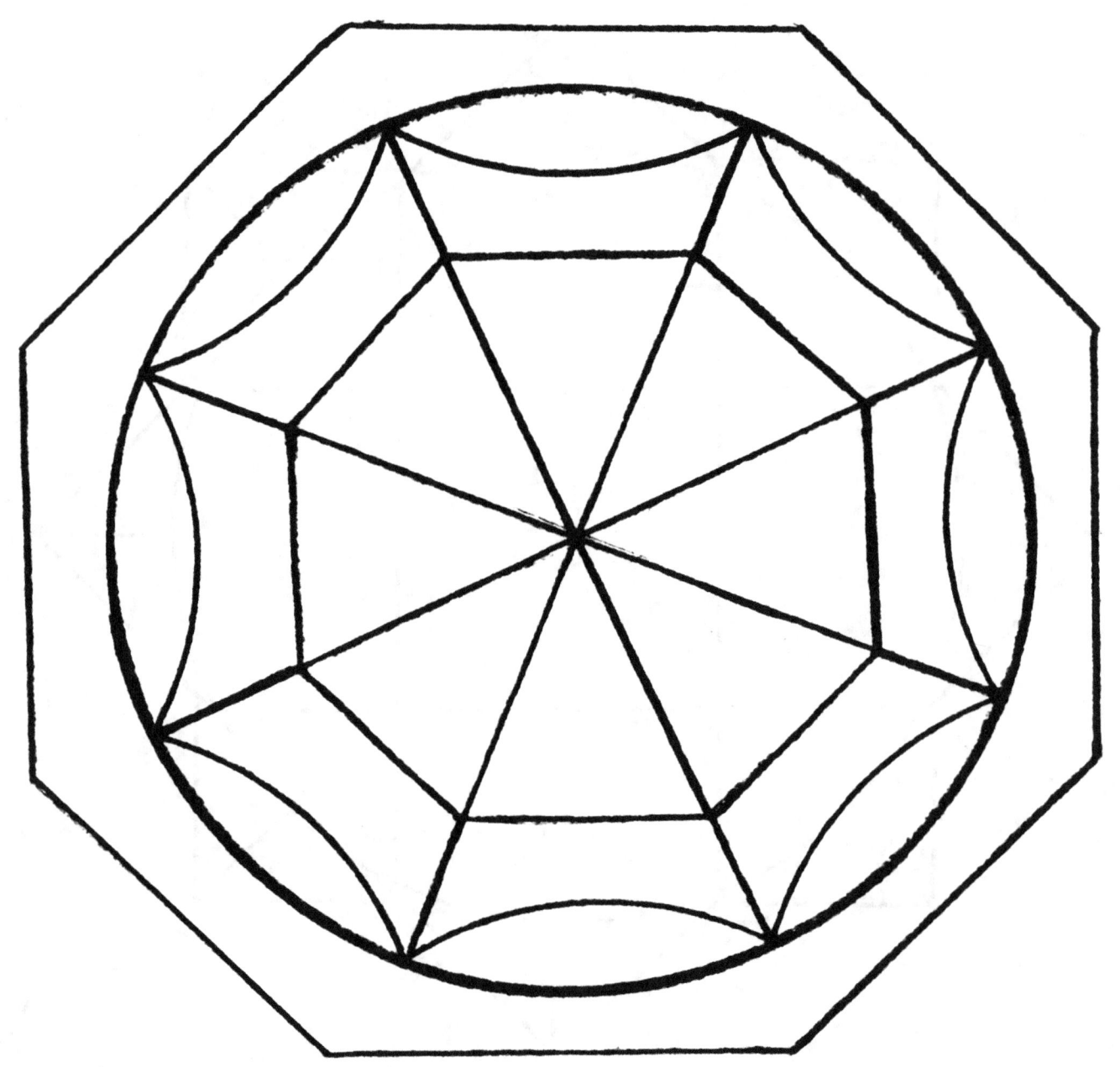

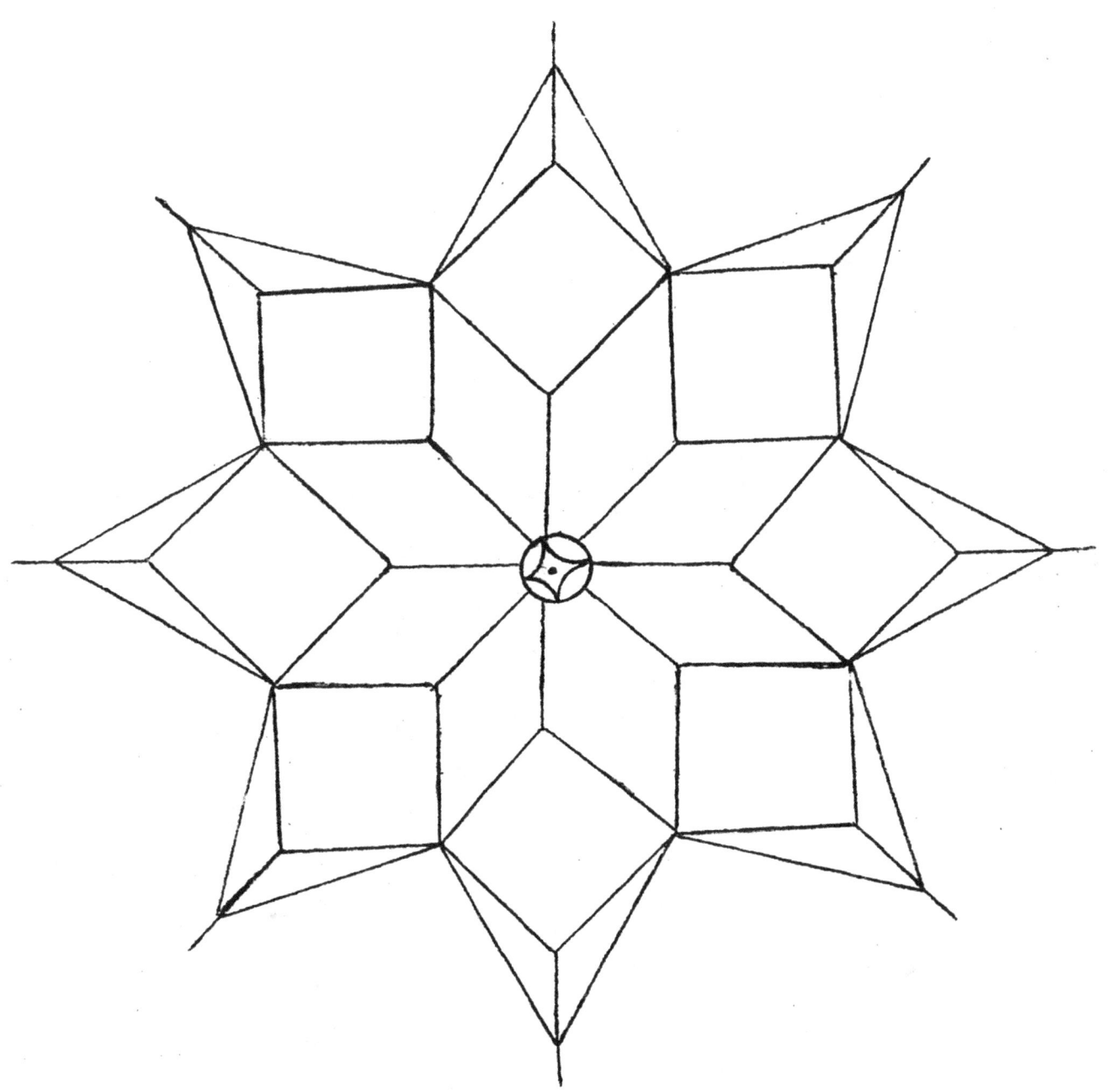

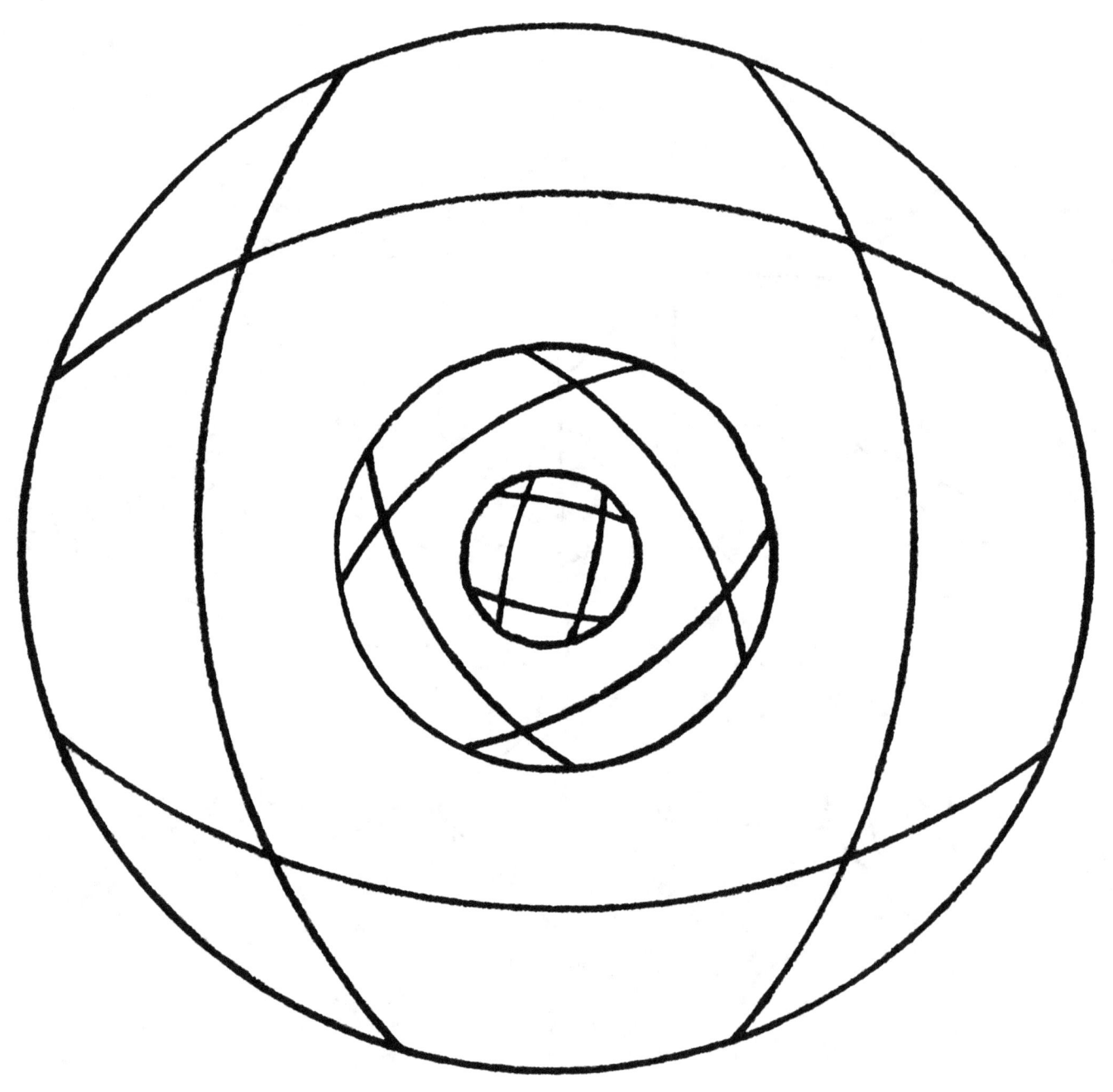

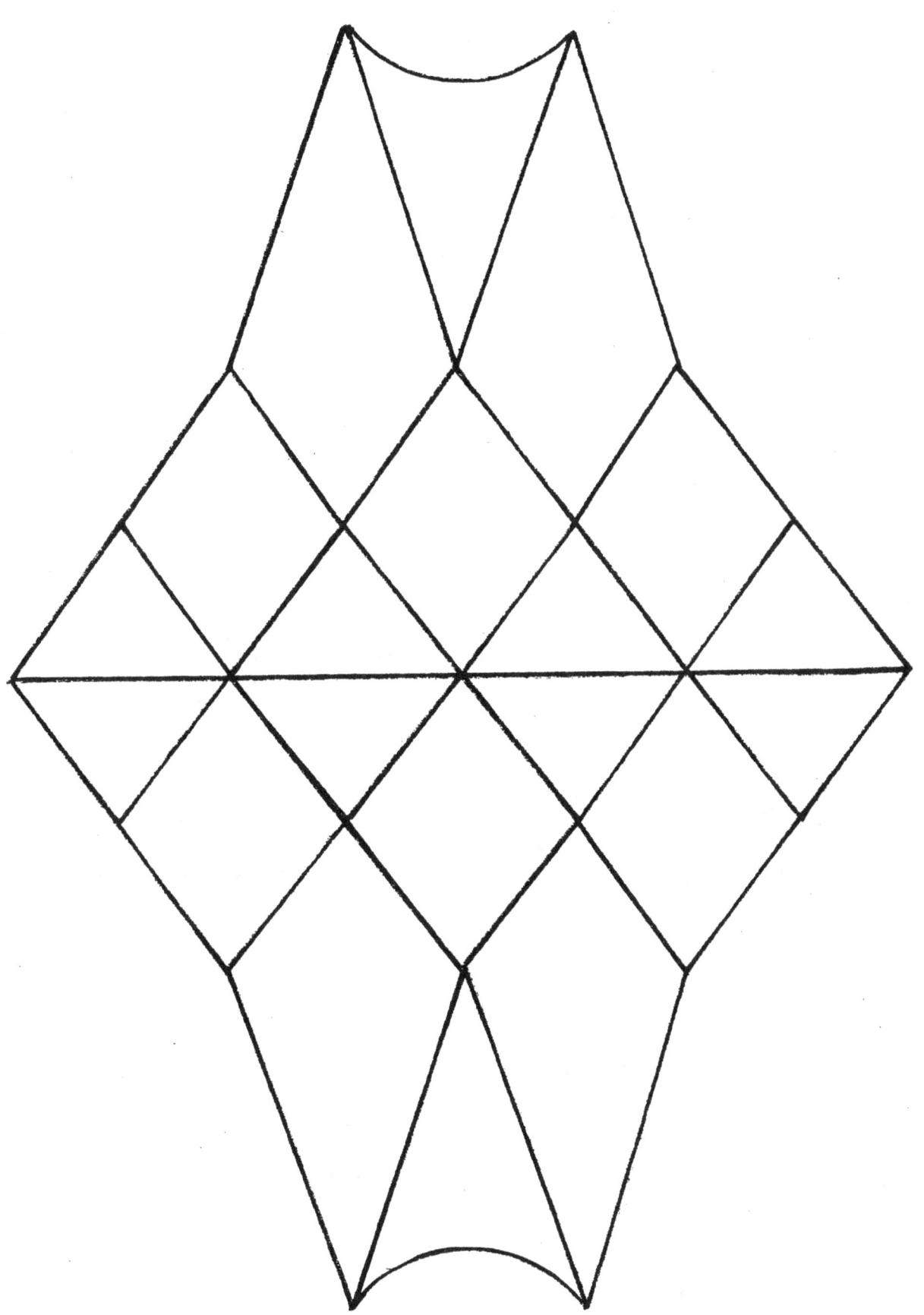

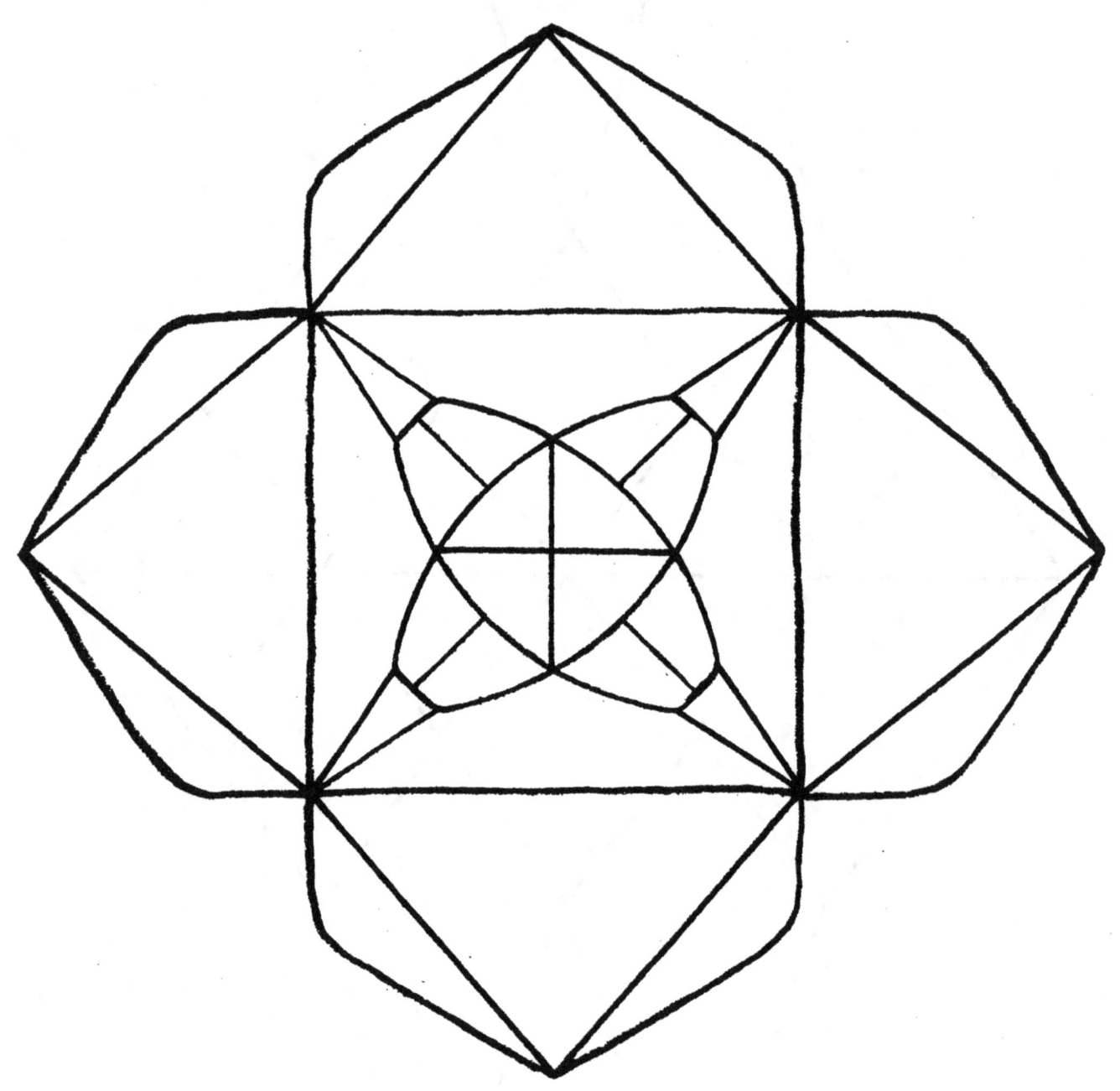

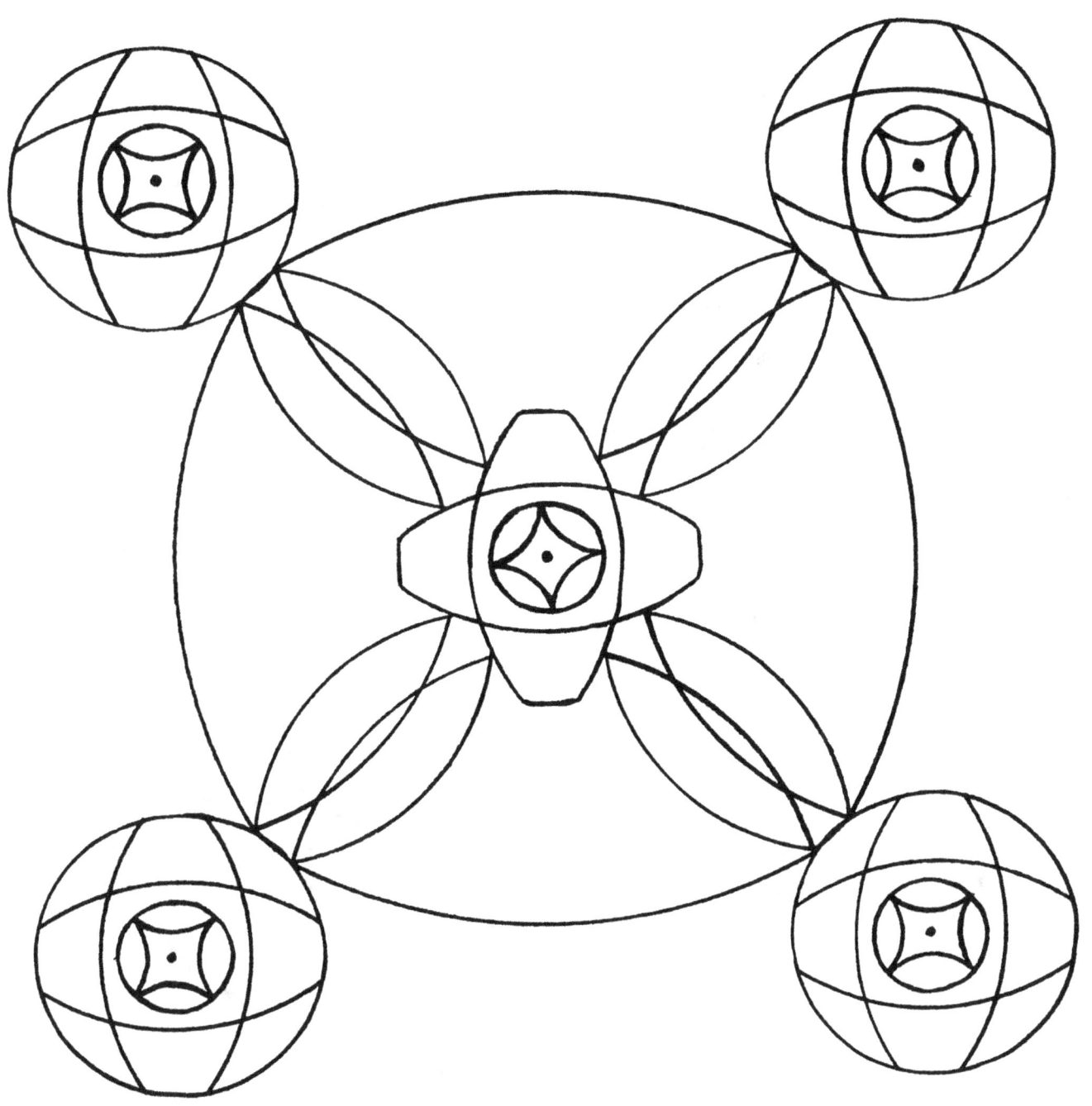

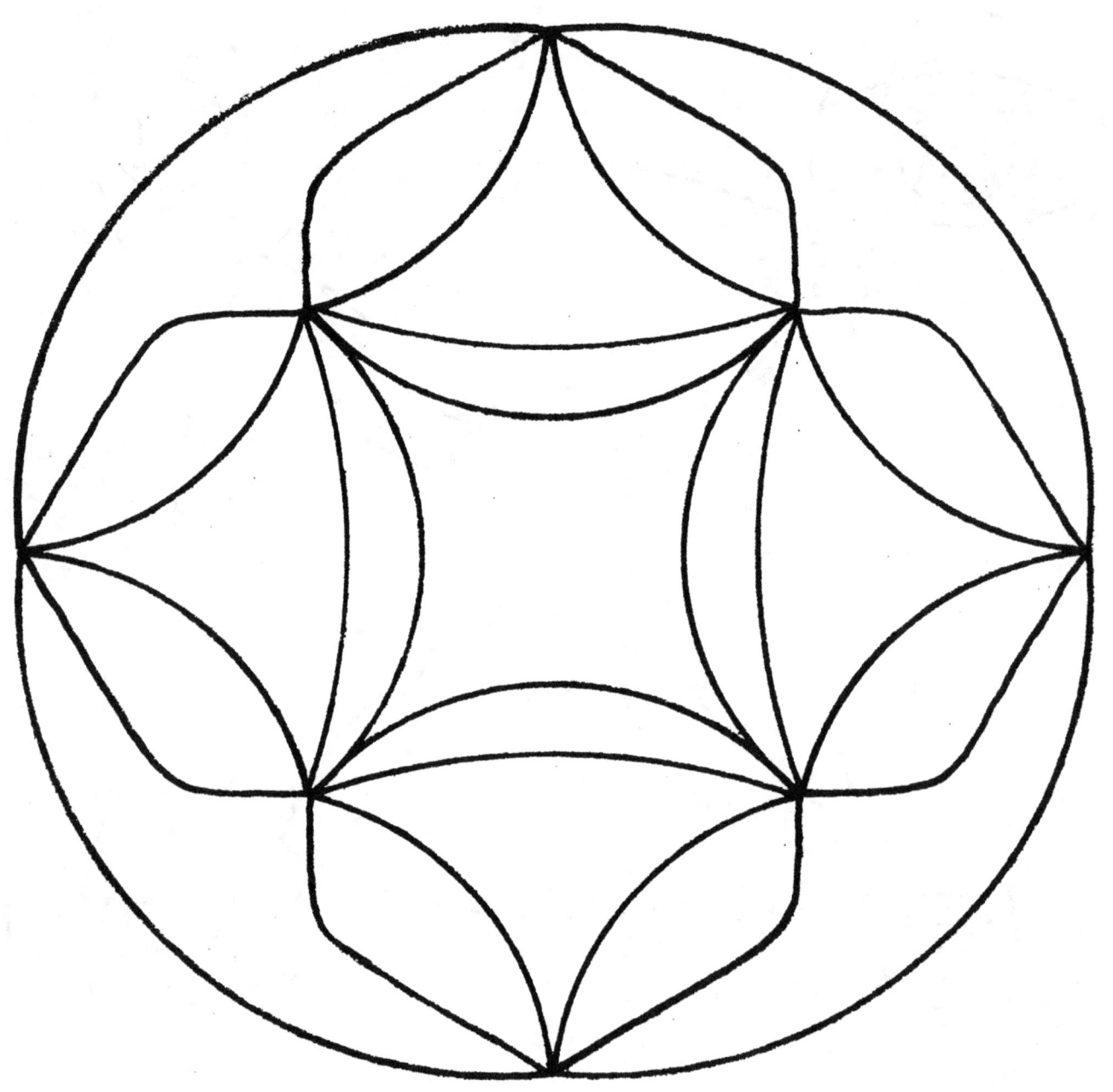

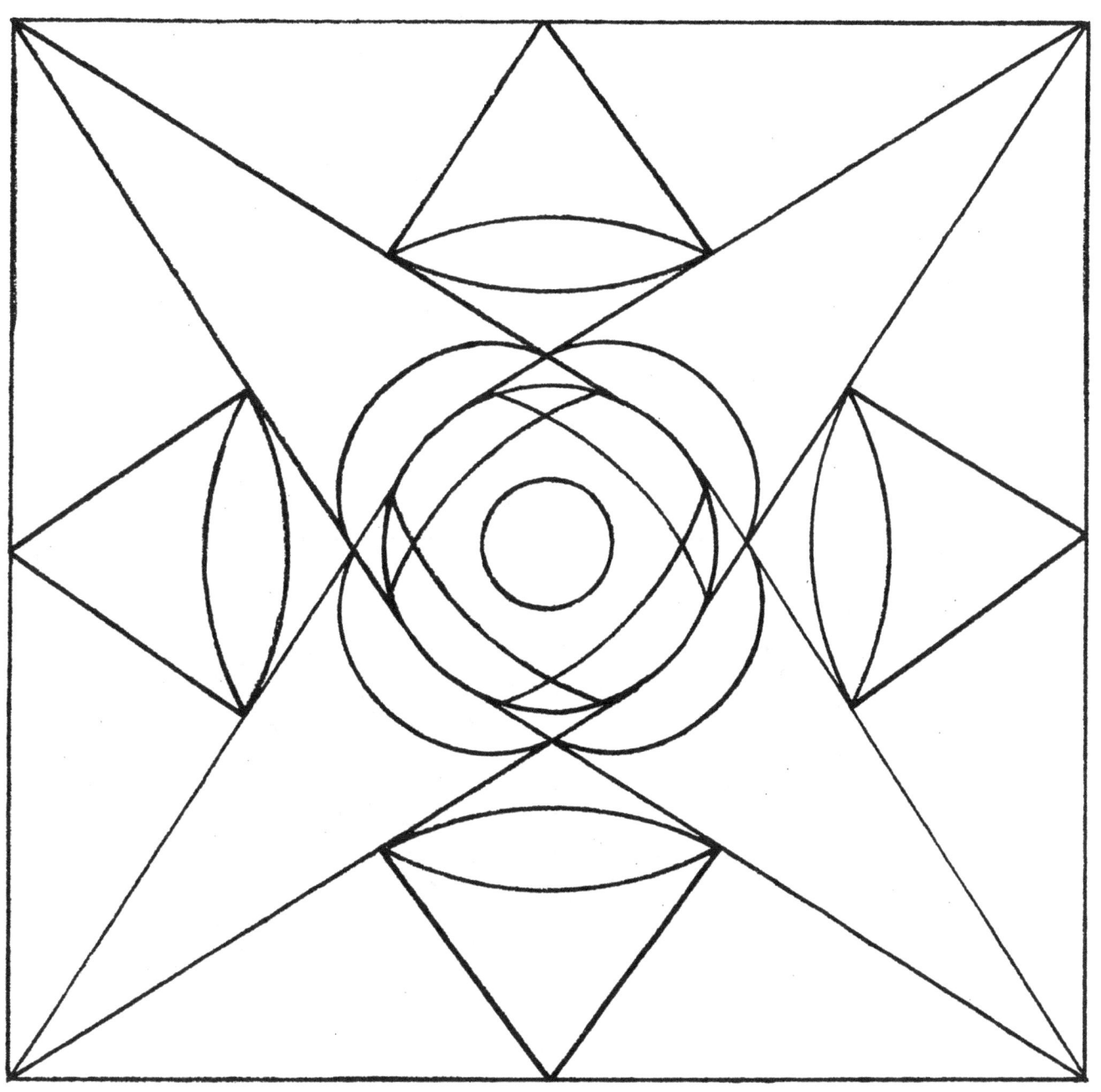

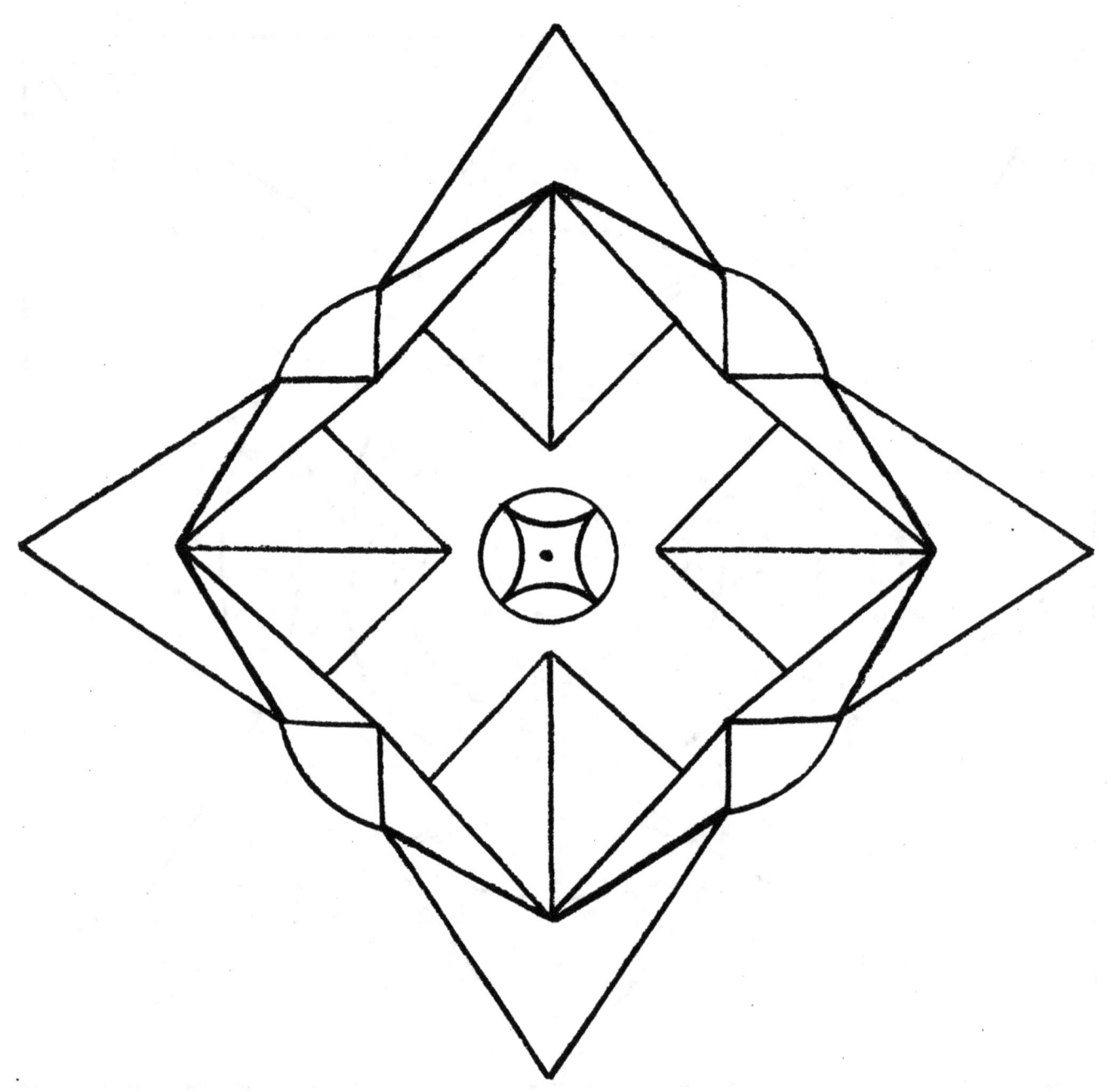